Fathers Day
1987
from Bill
&
Amy

AND THE LAUGH SHALL BE FIRST

AND THE

LAUGH

SHALL BE FIRST

a treasury of religious humor

compiled by
WILLIAM H. WILLIMON

ABINGDON PRESS
Nashville

AND THE LAUGH SHALL BE FIRST
A Treasury of Religious Humor

Copyright © 1986 by Abingdon Press

Second Printing 1986

This book is printed on acid-free paper.

Library of Congress Cataloging-in-Publication Data

And the laugh shall be first, a treasury of religious humor.

1. Christianity and humor. I. Willimon, William H.
BR115.H84A53   1986   202'.07   86-7851

ISBN 0-687-01383-6

Scripture quotations unless otherwise noted are from the
Revised Standard Version of the Bible, copyrighted 1946,
1952, © 1971, 1973 by the Division of Christian Education of
the National Council of the Churches of Christ in the
U.S.A., and used by permission.

MANUFACTURED BY THE PARTHENON PRESS AT
NASHVILLE, TENNESSEE, UNITED STATES OF AMERICA

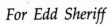
For Edd Sheriff

"SOUR GODLINESS IS THE DEVIL'S RELIGION."

John Wesley

No morons so play the fool as those who are obsessed with the ardor of Christian piety to the point that they distribute their goods, overlook injuries, suffer themselves to be deceived, make no distinction between friends and enemies, eschew pleasure, glut themselves with hunger, vigils, tears, toils, and reproaches, who disdain life, who crave only death, who seem utterly to contemn all common sense, as if the soul lived elsewhere and not in the body. What is this if not insanity? No wonder that the apostles appeared to be drunk with new wine and Paul seemed to Festus to be mad. Christ himself became a fool when he was found in fashion as a man that he might bring healing by the foolishness of the cross. 'For God has chosen the foolish things of the world to confound the wise, and the weak things of the world to confound the mighty.'

Erasmus, *The Praise of Folly, 1509*

CONTENTS

INTRODUCTION

Among all of God's creatures, human beings are the only animals who both laugh and weep—for we are the only animals who are struck with the difference between the way things are and the way things ought to be. In those priceless moments when we are struck with the incongruity of this world, humor results. A stern, smug gentleman slips on a banana peel and ends up sprawled on the sidewalk; W. C. Fields throws a pie in the face of a haughty woman in an evening gown; a mischievous peasant puts the cruel landlord in his place—we laugh.

In these moments when the human situation is exposed, when the so-deadly-serious ones are made to look like fools, Christians sing with Mary before us that such fun is the divine result of a God who,

> has scattered the proud in the imagination of their hearts,
> . . . has put down the mighty from their thrones,
> and exalted those of low degree. (*Luke 1:51-52*)

Humor occurs when we are put in our place.

Justice occurs, says the Bible, when God puts all of us in our place, when the first end up last and the last move to the front of the line. Thus, there is something fundamentally righteous and holy about our humor. Christians who like to think of themselves as so serious about justice, so concerned about the attainment of goodness, are often guilty of taking themselves too seriously, of ascribing too much good to their own efforts, their ideals, their righteous indignation. Thus, Reinhold Niebuhr says somewhere that the very essence of sin is to take ourselves too seriously.

If that be true, then the very essence of grace is to receive the gift of laughter, especially when the joke is on us, particularly when the most laughable incongruities consist of the gap between who we are and who God would have us to be.

Of course, there is humor that is cruel—sarcasm, ridicule, derision. Ethnic jokes, racist slurs, and sacrilegious ridicule represent humor perverted, humor turned serious in the service of bigotry and pride. There is nothing funny in this.

Yet, even in justice, as God's lifting up those of low degree involves the pain of someone having to come down, there is an inevitably dark side to even the most gentle and gracious humor. All laughter occurs in the space between what is and what ought to be, in the gracious no-man's-land somewhere betwixt how we view ourselves and how we really appear. There is truth in all good humor, a truth so true, often so painfully true, that we nervously laugh, aware that we are not at all accustomed to seeing ourselves as we are—clowns and fools rather than heroes and saints.

Perhaps because such truth always wavers between wearing the mask of comedy or that of tragedy, perhaps because the truth invariably hurts somebody, people often avoid humor—particularly church people. In church, we confront so many serious problems—sin, injustice, hunger, ignorance, hate, war. How dare someone laugh in the midst of our seriousness? In church, we confront the things of God. Where is there a place for laughter in that?

But as Jesus' own critics demonstrated, good people, religious people, seriously devout people, are often those most prone to a seriousness which is nothing less than sinful. Whether liberal or conservative, in church with our moral checklist of peccadilloes, our anxious self-examination, our nervous desire always to be right, always to be found pure, correct in word and deed, we don't need God to save us. We are busy saving ourselves. How dare some upstart poke fun at our righteousness! So Nietzsche says that "The devil is the spirit of gravity."

Both revolutionaries and tyrants are noted for their humorlessness. Is this so surprising? The tyrant cannot tolerate any suggestion that he or she is not invincible, omnipotent, and right. The revolutionary cannot stand the notion that perhaps, just perhaps, the revolution is filled with a host of mixed motives and the results will be as mixed as the tyranny the revolution seeks to overthrow. All good humor is seditious to the presumptions of both revolutionaries and the establishment. Humorists are among the first to go underground in the totalitarian state. They go underground but they can never be fully silenced. The human inclination to overcome it all with a snicker is virtually indomitable, thank God.

Today, as always, most of the really good comedians come from the ranks of the oppressed. "You can keep me poor and powerless," they seem to say, "but you will never keep me from laughing."

This book is a collection of my favorite contemporary religious humor and satire. Of course, it is not an exhaustive treatment. By contemporary, you will see that I mean from Mark Twain to the present. By religious, I mean mostly Protestant humorists from the United States. Each selection, in its own way, is a kind of testimony to the vitality of the human spirit, the amazing ability of the human animal to laugh even at what it holds most dear, especially at what it holds most dear. Each piece has theological significance, though not as we often think of theology—the dry, dull enterprise of academicians. Here is the gracious, witty, perceptive theology of the holy fool who enables us to look at ourselves in new and fresh ways, to smile at our shortcomings rather than merely to wring our hands and weep, and to enjoy ourselves, even as God must sometimes enjoy us.

I have selected each piece so that it can be read easily at one sitting. Each selection should be able to stand on its own without reference to other material, save the short introduction at the beginning.

I hope that this collection of humor and satire will provide many hours of insight and grace—two essential commodities in perennial short supply, in church or out.

William H. Willimon
Duke University Chapel
Advent, 1985

1

We begin with the most famous of American humorists, Mark Twain. This selection from The Innocents Abroad *is Twain at his skeptical best, an uproarious clash of modern reason and science with the credulity of the old world. For Twain, the future lies with the American innocents whose commonsense pragmatism and distrust of tradition enable them to poke fun at the superstitious practices of an Age of Belief which was passing away.*

AT ADAM'S TOMB*

Mark Twain

The Greek chapel is the most roomy, the richest and the showiest chapel in the Church of the Holy Sepulchre. Its altar, like that of all the Greek churches, is a lofty screen that extends clear across the chapel, and is gorgeous with gilding and pictures. The numerous lamps that hang before it are of gold and silver, and cost great sums.

But the feature of the place is a short column that rises from the middle of the marble pavement of the chapel and marks the exact *center of the earth*. The most reliable traditions tell us that this was known to be the earth's center, ages ago, and that when Christ was upon earth he set all doubts upon the subject at rest forever by stating with his own lips that the tradition was correct. Remember, he said that that particular column stood upon the center of the world. If the center of the world changes, the column changes its position accordingly. This column has

*From *The Innocents Abroad.*

moved three different times of its own accord. This is because, in great convulsions of nature, at three different times, masses of the earth—whole ranges of mountains, probably—have flown off into space, thus lessening the diameter of the earth and changing the exact locality of its center by a point or two. This is a very curious and interesting circumstance, and is a withering rebuke to those philosophers who would make us believe that it is not possible for any portion of the earth to fly off into space.

To satisfy himself that this spot was really the center of the earth, a skeptic once paid well for the privilege of ascending to the dome of the church to see if the sun gave him a shadow at noon. He came down perfectly convinced. The day was very cloudy and the sun threw no shadows at all; but the man was satisfied that if the sun had come out and made shadows it could not have made any for him. Proofs like these are not to be set aside by the idle tongues of cavilers. To such as are not bigoted and are willing to be convinced, they carry a conviction that nothing can ever shake.

If even greater proofs than those I have mentioned are wanted, to satisfy the headstrong and the foolish that this is the genuine center of the earth, they are here. The greatest of them lies in the fact that from under this very column was taken the *dust from which Adam was made.* This can surely be regarded in the light of a settler. It is not likely that the original first man would have been made from an inferior quality of earth when it was entirely convenient to get first quality from the world's center. This will strike any reflecting mind forcibly. That Adam was formed of dirt procured in this very spot is amply proven by the fact that in six thousand years no man has ever been able to prove that the dirt was *not* procured here whereof he was made.

It is a singular circumstance that right under the roof of this same great church, and not far away from that illustrious column, Adam himself, the father of the human race, lies buried. There is no question that he is actually buried in the grave which is pointed out as his—there can be none—because it has never yet been proven that that grave is not the grave in which he is buried.

The tomb of Adam! How touching it was, here in a land of strangers, far away from home and friends and all who cared for me, thus to discover the grave of a blood relation. True, a distant one, but still a relation. The unerring instinct of nature thrilled its recognition. The fountain of my filial affection was stirred to its profoundest depths, and I gave way to tumultuous emotion. I leaned upon a pillar and burst into tears. I deem it no shame to have wept over the grave of my poor dead relative. Let him who would sneer at my emotion close this volume here, for he will find little to his taste in my journeyings through Holy Land. Noble old man—he did not live to see me—he did not live to see his child. And I— I— alas, I did not live to see *him*. Weighed down by sorrow and disappointment, he died before I was born—six thousand brief summers before I was born. But let us try to bear it with fortitude. Let us trust that he is better off where he is. Let us take comfort in the thought that his loss is our eternal gain.

2

The unscrupulous, conniving, loud mouth Reverend Elmer Gantry has become the indelible image of religious hypocrisy and shame. In his 1927 novel, Sinclair Lewis stung American evangelical religion to its core. Never again could an American look upon a religious huckster without thinking of the escapades of Elmer.

In this passage from the novel, Elmer has decided that what the town of Zenith needs is a good, fire breathing, self-righteous crusade, led of course, by Elmer himself. He calls a meeting of the town's clergy to discuss the issue, and the meeting results in a biting commentary on conflicts and moral dilemmas within the ministry.

THE CLERGY MEET*

Sinclair Lewis

When he had been in Zenith for a year and three-quarters, Elmer formed the Committee on Public Morals, and conducted his raids on the red-light district.

It seemed to him that he was getting less publicity. Even his friend, Colonel Rutherford Snow, owner of the *Advocate-Times*, explained that just saying things couldn't go on being news; news was essentially a report of things done.

"All right, I'll *do* things, by golly, now that I've got Webster and Wink to take care of the glad hand for the brethren!" Elmer vowed.

He received an inspiration to the effect that all of a sudden, for reasons not defined, "things have gotten so bad in Zenith,

*From *Elmer Gantry* by Sinclair Lewis, copyright 1927 by Harcourt Brace Jovanovich, Inc.; renewed 1955 by Michael Lewis. Reprinted by permission of the publisher and with acknowledgments to the Sinclair Lewis Estate.

immorality is so rampant in high places and low, threatening the morals of youth and the sanctity of domesticity, that it is not enough for the ministry to stand back warning the malefactors, but a time now to come out of our dignified seclusion and personally wage open war on the forces of evil."

He said these startling things in the pulpit, he said them in an interview, and he said them in a letter to the most important clergymen in town, inviting them to meet with him to form a Committee on Public Morals and make plans for open war.

The devil must have been shaken. Anyway, the newspapers said that the mere threat of the formation of the Committee had caused "a number of well-known crooks and women of bad reputation to leave town." Who these scoundrels were, the papers did not say.

The Committee was to be composed of the Reverends Elmer Gantry and Otto Hickenlooper, Methodists; G. Prosper Edwards, Congregationalist; John Jennison Drew, Presbyterian; Edmund St. Vincent Zahn, Lutheran; James F. Gomer, Disciples; Father Matthew Smeesby, Catholic; Bernard Amos, Jewish; Hosea Jessup, Baptist; Willis Fortune Tate, Episcopalian; and Irving Tillish, Christian Science reader; with Wallace Umstead, the Y.M.C.A. secretary, four moral laymen, and a lawyer, Mr. T. J. Rigg.

They assembled at lunch in a private dining-room at the palatial Zenith Athletic Club. Being clergymen, and having to prove that they were also red-blooded, as they gathered before lunch in the lobby of the club they were particularly boisterous in shouting to passing acquaintances, florists and doctors and wholesale plumbers. To one George Babbitt, a real estate man, Dr. Drew, the Presbyterian, clamored, "Hey, Georgie! Got a flask along? Lunching with a bunch of preachers, and I reckon they'll want a drink!"

There was a great admiration on the part of Mr. Babbitt, and laughter among all the clergymen, except the Episcopal Mr. Tate and the Christian Scientific Mr. Tillish.

The private dining-room at the club was a thin red apartment with two pictures of young Indian maidens of Lithuanian origin sitting in native costumes, which gave free play to their legs,

17

under a rugged pine-tree against a background of extremely high mountains. In Private Dining-room A, beside them, was a lunch of the Men's Furnishers Association, addressed by S. Garrison Siegel of New York on "The Rented Dress Suit Business and How to Run It in a High-class Way."

The incipient Committee on Public Morals sat about a long narrow table in bent-wood chairs, in which they were always vainly trying to tilt back. Their table did not suggest debauchery and the demon rum. There were only chilly and naked-looking goblets of ice water.

They lunched, gravely, on consommé, celery, roast lamb, which was rather cold, mashed potatoes, which were arctic, Brussels sprouts, which were overstewed, ice cream, which was warm; with very large cups of coffee, and no smoking afterward.

Elmer began, "I don't know who is the oldest among us, but certainly no one in this room has had a more distinguished or more valuable term of Christian service than Dr. Edwards, of Pilgrim Congregational, and I know you'll join me in asking him to say grace before meat."

The table conversation was less cheerful than the blessing.

They all detested one another. Every one knew of some case in which each of the others had stolen, or was said to have tried to steal, some parishioner, to have corrupted his faith and appropriated his contributions. Dr. Hickenlooper and Dr. Drew had each advertised that he had the largest Sunday School in the city. All of the Protestants wanted to throw ruinous questions about the Immaculate Conception at Father Smeesby, and Father Smeesby, a smiling dark man of forty, had ready, in case they should attack the Catholic Church, the story of the ant who said to the elephant, "Move over, who do you think you're pushing?" All of them, except Mr. Tillish, wanted to ask Mr. Tillish how he'd ever been fooled by this charlatan, Mary Baker Eddy, and all of them, except the rabbi, wanted to ask Rabbi Amos why the Jews were such numbskulls as not to join the Christian faith.

They were dreadfully cordial. They kept their voices bland, and smiled too often, and never listened to one another. Elmer, aghast, saw that they would flee before making an organization if he did not draw them together. And what was the one thing in which they were all joyously interested? Why, vice! He'd begin the vice rampage now, instead of waiting till the business meeting after lunch.

He pounded on the table, and demanded, "Most of you have been in Zenith longer than myself. I admit ignorance. It is true that I have unearthed many dreadful, *dreadful* cases of secret sin. But you gentlemen, who know the town so much better—Am I right? Are Conditions as dreadful as I think, or do I exaggerate?"

All of them lighted up and, suddenly looking on Elmer as a really nice man after all, they began happily to tell of their woeful discoveries. . . . The blood-chilling incident of the father who found in the handbag of his sixteen-year-old daughter improper pictures. The suspicion that at a dinner of war veterans at the Leroy House there had danced a young lady who wore no garments save slippers and a hat.

"I know all about that dinner—I got the details from a man in my church—I'll tell you about it if you feel you ought to know," said Dr. Gomer.

They looked as though they decidedly felt that they ought to know. He went into details, very, and at the end Dr. Jessup gulped, "Oh, that Leroy House is absolutely a den of iniquity! It ought to be pulled!"

"It certainly ought to! I don't think I'm cruel," shouted Dr. Zahn, the Lutheran, "but if I had my way, I'd burn the proprietor of that joint at the stake!"

All of them had incidents of shocking obscenity all over the place—all of them except Father Smeesby, who sat back and smiled, the Episcopal Dr. Tate, who sat back and looked bored, and Mr. Tillish, the healer, who sat back and looked chilly. In fact it seemed as though, despite the efforts of themselves and the thousands of other inspired and highly trained Christian ministers who had worked over it ever since its foundation, the city of Zenith was another Sodom. But the alarmed apostles did not appear to be so worried as they said they were. They listened with almost benign attention while Dr. Zahn, in his

German accent, told of alarming crushes between the society girls whom he knew so well from dining once a year with his richest parishioner.

They were all, indeed, absorbed in vice to a degree gratifying to Elmer.

But at the time for doing something about it, for passing resolutions and appointing sub-committees and outlining programs, they drew back.

"Can't we all get together—pool our efforts?" pleaded Elmer. "Whatever our creedal differences, surely we stand alike in worshiping the same God and advocating the same code of morals. I'd like to see this Committee as a permanent organization, and finally, when the time is ripe—Think how it would jolt the town! All of us getting ourselves appointed special police or deputy sheriffs, and personally marching down on these abominations, arresting the blood-guilty wretches, and putting them where they can do no harm! Maybe leading our church members in the crusade! Think of it!"

They did think of it, and they were alarmed.

Father Smeesby spoke. "My church, gentlemen, probably has a more rigid theology than yours, but I don't think we're quite so alarmed by discovering the fact, which seems to astonish you, that sinners often sin. The Catholic Church may be harder to believe, but it's easier to live with."

"My organization," said Mr. Tillish, "could not think of joining in a wild witch-hunt, any more than we could in indiscriminate charity. For both the poverty-laden and the vicious—" He made a little whistling between his beautiful but false teeth, and went on with frigid benignancy. "For all such, the truth is clearly stated in 'Science and Health' and made public in all our meetings—the truth that both vice and poverty, like sickness, are unreal, are errors, to be got rid of by understanding that God is All-in-all; that disease, death, evil, sin deny good, omnipotent God, life. Well! If these so-called sufferers do not care to take the truth when it is freely offered them, is that our fault? I understand your sympathy with the unfortunate, but you are not going to put out ignorance by fire."

"Golly, let me crawl too," chuckled Rabbi Amos. "If you want to get a vice-crusading rabbi, get one of these smart-aleck young liberals from the Cincinnati school—and they'll mostly have too much sympathy with the sinners to help you either! Anyway, my congregation is so horribly respectable that if their rabbi did anything but sit in his study and look learned, they'd kick him out."

"And I," said Dr. Willis Fortune Tate, of St. Colomb's Episcopal, "if you will permit me to say so, can regard such a project as our acting like policemen and dealing with these malefactors in person as nothing short of vulgar, as well as useless. I understand your high ideals, Dr. Gantry—"

"Mr. Gantry."

"—Mr. Gantry, and I honor you for them, and respect your energy, but I beg you to consider how the press and the ordinary laity, with their incurably common and untrained minds, would misunderstand."

"I'm afraid I must agree with Dr. Tate," said the Congregational Dr. G. Prosper Edwards, in the manner of the Pilgrim's Monument agreeing with Westminster Abbey.

And as for the others, they said they really must "take time and think it over," and they all got away as hastily and cordially as they could.

Elmer walked with his friend and pillar, Mr. T. J. Rigg, toward the dentist's office in which even an ordained minister of God would shortly take on strangely normal writhings and gurglings.

"They're a fine bunch of sacred prophets, a noble lot of apostolic ice-cream cones!" protested Mr. Rigg. "Hard luck, Brother Elmer! I'm sorry. It really is good stuff, this vice-crusading. Oh, I don't suppose it makes the slightest difference in the amount of vice—and I don't know that it ought to make any. Got to give fellows that haven't our advantages some chance to let off steam. But it does get the church a lot of attention. I'm mightly proud of the way we're building up Wellspring Church again. Kind of a hobby with me. But makes me indignant, these spiritual cold-storage eggs not supporting you!"

But as he looked up he saw that Elmer was grinning.

"I'm not worried, T. J. Fact, I'm tickled to death. First place, I've scared 'em off the subject of vice. Before they get back to preaching about it, I'll have the whole subject absolutely patented for our church. And now they won't have the nerve to imitate me if I do do this personal crusading stunt. Third, I can preach against 'em! And I will! You watch me! Oh, not mention any names—no come-back—but tell 'em how I pleaded with a gang of preachers to take practical methods to end immorality, and they were all scared!"

"Fine!" said the benevolent trustee. "We'll let 'em know that Wellspring is the one church that's really following the gospel."

"We sure will! Now listen, T. J.: if you trustees will stand for the expense, I want to get a couple of good private detectives or something, and have 'em dig up a lot of real addresses of places that *are* vicious—there must be some of 'em—and get some evidence. Then I'll jump on the police for not having pinched these places. I'll say they're so wide open that the police *must* know of 'em. And probably that's true, too. Man! A sensation! Run our disclosures every Sunday evening for a month! Make the chief of police try to answer us in the press!"

"Good stuff! Well, I know a fellow—he was a government man, prohibition agent, and got fired for boozing and blackmail. He's not exactly a double-crosser, lot straighter than most prohibition agents, but still I think he could slip us some real addresses. I'll have him see you."

22

3

No journalist ever wielded a more poisonous pen with more verbal ingenuity than H. L. Mencken. For decades Mencken waged unceasing war against American "boobism" and "buncombe" wherever he found it—particularly in the world of fundamentalist religion. "The Hills of Zion" was written when he was covering the Scopes trial at Dayton, Tennessee, for the Baltimore Evening Sun *in July 1925. In this dispatch, he captures some of the ironies and humor in the clash between fundamentalism and modernism in a little Tennessee town.*

"THE HILLS OF ZION"*

H. L. Mencken

It was hot weather when they tried the infidel Scopes at Dayton, but I went down there very willingly, for I had good reports of the sub-Potomac bootleggers, and moreover I was eager to see something of evangelical Christianity as a going concern. In the big cities of the Republic, despite the endless efforts of consecrated men, it is laid up with a wasting disease. The very Sunday-school superintendents, taking jazz from the stealthy radio, shake their fire-proof legs; their pupils, moving into adolescence, no longer respond to the proliferating hormones by enlisting for missionary service in Africa, but resort to necking and petting instead. I know of no evangelical church from Oregon to Maine that is not short of money: the graft begins to peter out, like wire-tapping and three-card monte before it. Even in Dayton, though the mob was up to do execution upon Scopes, there was a strong smell of antinomianism. The nine churches of the village were all half empty on Sunday, and weeds choked their yards. Only two or three of the resident pastors managed to sustain themselves by their ghostly science; the rest had to take orders from mail-order pantaloons or work in the adjacent strawberry fields; one, I heard, was a barber. On the courthouse green a score of sweating theologians debated the darker passages of Holy Writ day and night, but I soon found that they were all volunteers, and that the local faithful, while interested in their exegesis as an intellectual exercise, did not permit it to impede the indigenous debaucheries. Exactly twelve minutes after I reached the village I was taken in tow by a Christian man and introduced to the favorite tipple of the Cumberland Range: half corn liquor and half coca-cola. It seemed a dreadful dose to me, spoiled as I was by the bootleg light wines and beers of the Eastern seaboard, but I found that the Dayton illuminati got it down with gusto, rubbing their tummies and rolling their eyes. I include among them the chief local proponents of the Mosaic cosmogony. They were all hot for Genesis, but their faces were far too florid to belong to teetotalers, and when a pretty girl came tripping down the Main street, which was very often, they reached for the places where their neckties should have been with all the amorous enterprise of movie actors. It seemed somehow strange.

An amiable newspaper woman of Chattanooga, familiar with those uplands, presently enlightened me. Dayton, she explained, was simply a great capital like any other great capital. That is to say, it was to Rhea county what Atlanta was to Georgia or Paris to France. That is to say, it was predominantly epicurean and sinful. A country girl from some remote valley of the county, coming into town for her semi-annual bottle of Lydia Pinkham's Vegetable Compound, shivered on approaching Robinson's drug-store quite as a country girl from up-State New York might shiver on approaching the Metropolitan Opera House or the Ritz Hotel. In every village lout she saw a potential white-slaver. The hard sidewalks hurt her feet.

Temptations of the flesh bristled to all sides of her, luring her to hell. This newspaper woman told me of a session with just such a visitor, holden a few days before. The latter waited outside one of the town hot-dog and coca-cola shops while her husband negotiated with a hardware merchant across the street. The newspaper woman, idling along and observing that the stranger was badly used by the heat, invited her to step into the shop for a glass of coca-cola. The invitation brought forth only a gurgle of terror. Coca-cola, it quickly appeared, was prohibited by the country lady's pastor, as a levantine and hell-sent narcotic. He also prohibited coffee and tea—and pies! He had his doubts about white bread and boughten meat. The newspaper woman, interested, inquired about ice-cream. It was, she found, not specifically prohibited, but going into a coca-cola shop to get it would be clearly sinful. So she offered to get a saucer of it, and bring it out to the sidewalk. The visitor vacillated—and came near being lost. But God saved her in the nick of time. When the newspaper woman emerged from the place she was in full flight up the street! Later on her husband, mounted on a mule, overtook her four miles out the mountain pike.

This newspaper woman, whose kindness covered city infidels as well as Alpine Chistians, offered to take me back in the hills to a place where the old-time religion was genuinely on tap. The Scopes jury, she explained was composed mainly of its customers, with a few Dayton sophisticates added to leaven the mass. It would thus be instructive to climb the heights and observe the former at their ceremonies. The trip, fortunately, might be made by automobile. There was a road running out of Dayton to Morgantown, in the mountains to the westward, and thence beyond. But foreigners, it appeared, would have to approach the sacred grove cautiously, for the upland worshipers were very shy, and at the first sight of a strange face they would adjourn their orgy and slink into the forest. They were not to be feared, for God had long since forbidden them to practice assassination, or even assault, but if they were alarmed a rough trip would go for naught. So, after dreadful bumpings up a long and narrow road, we parked our car in a little woodpath a mile or two beyond the tiny village of Morgantown, and made the rest of the approach on foot, deployed like skirmishers. Far off in a dark, romantic glade a flickering light was visible, and out of the silence came the rumble of exhortation. We could distinguish the figure of the preacher only as a moving mote in the light: it was like looking down the tube of a dark-field microscope. Slowly and cautiously we crossed what seemed to be a pasture, and then we crouched down along the edge of a cornfield, and stealthily edged further and further. The light now grew larger and we could begin to make out what was going on. We went ahead on all fours, like snakes in the grass.

From the great limb of a mighty oak hung a couple of crude torches of the sort that car inspectors thrust under Pullman cars when a train pulls in at night. In the guttering glare was the preacher, and for a while we could see no one else. He was an immensely tall and thin mountaineer in blue jeans, his collarless shirt open at the neck and his hair a tousled mop. As he preached he paced up and down under the smoking flambeaux, and at each turn he thrust his arms into the air and yelled "Glory to God!" We crept nearer in the shadow of the cornfield, and began to hear more of his discourse. He was preaching on the Day of Judgment. The high kings of the earth, he roared, would all fall down and die; only the sanctified would stand up to receive the Lord God of Hosts. One of these kings he mentioned by name, the king of what he called Greece-y. The king of Greece-y, he said, was doomed to hell. We crawled forward a few more yards and began to see the audience. It was seated on benches ranged round the preacher in a circle. Behind him sat a row of elders, men and women. In front were the younger folk. We crept on cautiously, and individuals rose out of the ghostly gloom. A young mother sat suckling her baby, rocking as the preacher paced up and down. Two scared little girls hugged each other, their pigtails down their backs. An immensely huge mountain woman, in a gingham dress, cut in one piece, rolled on her heels at every "Glory to God!" To one side, and but half

26

visible, was what appeared to be a bed. We found afterward that half a dozen babies were asleep upon it.

The preacher stopped at last, and there arose out of the darkness a woman with her hair pulled back into a little tight knot. She began so quietly that we couldn't hear what she said, but soon her voice rose resonantly and we could follow her. She was denouncing the reading of books. Some wandering book agent, it appeared, had come to her cabin and tried to sell her a specimen of his wares. She refused to touch it. Why, indeed, read a book? If what was in it was true, then everything in it was already in the Bible. If it was false, then reading it would imperil the soul. This syllogism from Caliph Omar complete, she sat down. There followed a hymn, led by a somewhat fat brother wearing silver-rimmed country spectacles. It droned on for half a dozen stanzas, and then the first speaker resumed the floor. He argued that the gift of tongues was real and that education was a snare. Once his children could read the Bible, he said, they had enough. Beyond lay only infidelity and damnation. Sin stalked the cities. Dayton itself was a Sodom. Even Morgantown had begun to forget God. He sat down, and a female aurochs in gingham got up. She began quietly, but soon was leaping and roaring, and it was hard to follow her. Under cover of the turmoil we sneaked a bit closer.

A couple of other discourses followed, and there were two or three hymns. Suddenly a change of mood began to make itself felt. The last hymn ran longer than the others, and dropped gradually into a monotonous, unintelligible chant. The leader beat time with his book. The faithful broke out with exultations. When the singing ended there was a brief palaver that we could not hear, and two of the men moved a bench into the circle of light directly under the flambeaux. Then a half-grown girl emerged from the darkness and threw herself upon it. We noticed with astonishment that she had bobbed hair. "This sister," said the leader, "has asked for prayers." We moved a bit closer. We could now see faces plainly, and hear every word. What followed quickly reached such heights of barbaric grotesquerie that it was hard to believe it real. At a signal all the faithful crowded up to the bench and began to pray—not in unison, but each for himself! At another they all fell on their knees, their arms over the penitent. The leader kneeled facing us, his head alternately thrown back dramatically or buried in his hands. Words spouted from his lips like bullets from a machine-gun—appeals to God to pull the penitent back out of hell, defiances of the demons of the air, a vast impassioned jargon of apocalyptic texts. Suddenly he rose to his feet, threw back his head and began to speak in tongues—blub-blub-blub, gurgle-gurgle-gurgle. His voice rose to a higher register. The climax was a shrill, inarticulate squawk, like that of a man throttled. He fell headlong across the pyramid of suppliants.

A comic scene? Somehow, no. The poor half-wits were too horribly in earnest. It was like peeping through a knothole at the writhings of people in pain. From the squirming and jabbering mass a young woman gradually detached herself—a woman not uncomely, with a pathetic homemade cap on her head. Her head jerked back, the veins of her neck swelled, and her fists went to her throat as if she were fighting for breath. She bent backward until she was like half a hoop. Then she suddenly snapped forward. We caught a flash of the whites of her eyes. Presently her whole body began to be convulsed—great throes that began at the shoulders and ended at the hips. She would leap to her feet, thrust her arms in air, and then hurl herself upon the heap. Her praying flattened out into a mere delirious caterwauling, like that of a Tom cat on a petting party. I describe the thing discreetly, and as a strict behaviorist. The lady's subjective sensations I leave to infidel pathologists, privy to the works of Ellis, Freud and Moll. Whatever they were, they were obviously not painful, for they were accompanied by vast heavings and gurglings of a joyful and even ecstatic nature. And they seemed to be contagious, too, for soon a second penitent, also female, joined the first, and then came a third, and a fourth, and a fifth. The last one had an extraordinary violent attack. She began with mild enough jerks of the head, but in a moment she was bounding all over the place, like a chicken with its head cut off. Every time her head came up, a stream of hosannas would issue out of it. Once she collided with a dark, undersized brother hitherto silent and stolid. Contact with her set him off as if he had been kicked by a mule. He leaped into the air, threw back his head, and began to gargle as if with a mouthful of BB shot. Then he loosed one tremendous, stentorian sentence in the tongues, and collapsed.

By this time the performers were quite oblivious of the profane universe and so it was safe to go still closer. We left our hiding and came up to the little circle of light. We slipped into the vacant seats on one of the rickety benches. The heap of mourners was directly before us. They bounced into us as they cavorted. The smell that they radiated, sweating there in that obscene heap, half suffocated us. Not all of them, of course, did the thing in the grand manner. Some merely moaned and rolled their eyes. The female ox in gingham flung her great bulk on the ground and jabbered an unintelligible prayer. One of the men, in the intervals between fits, put on his spectacles and read his Bible. Beside me on the bench sat the young mother and her baby. She suckled it through the whole orgy, obviously fascinated by what was going on, but never venturing to take any hand in it. On the bed just outside the light half a dozen other babies slept peacefully. In the shadows, suddenly appearing and as suddenly going away, were vague figures, whether of believers or of scoffers I do not know. They seemed to come and go in couples. Now and then a couple at the ringside would step out and vanish into the black night. After a while some came back, the males looking somewhat sheepish. There was whispering outside the circle of vision. A couple of Fords lurched up the road, cutting holes in the darkness with their lights. Once someone out of sight loosed a bray of laughter.

All this went on for an hour or so. The original penitent, by this time, was buried three deep beneath the heap. One caught a glimpse, now and then, of her yellow bobbed hair, but then she would vanish again. How she breathed down there I don't know; it was hard enough six feet away, with a strong five-cent cigar to help. When the praying brothers would rise up for a bout with the tongues their faces were streaming with perspiration. The fat harridan in gingham sweated like a longshoreman. Her hair got loose and fell down over her face. She fanned herself with her skirt. A powerful old gal she was, plainly equal in her day to a bout with obstetrics and a week's washing on the same morning, but this was worse than a week's washing. Finally, she fell into a heap, breathing in great, convulsive gasps.

Finally, we got tired of the show and returned to Dayton. It was nearly eleven o'clock—an immensely late hour for those latitudes—but the whole town was still gathered in the courthouse yard, listening to the disputes of theologians. The Scopes trial had brought them in from all directions. There was a friar wearing a sandwich sign announcing that he was the Bible champion of the world. There was a Seventh Day Adventist arguing that Clarence Darrow was the beast with seven heads and ten horns described in Revelation xiii, and that the end of the world was at hand. There was an evangelist made up like Andy Gump, with the news that atheists in Cincinnati were preparing to descend upon Dayton, hang the eminent Judge Raulston, and burn the town. There was an ancient who maintained that no Catholic could be a Christian. There was the eloquent Dr. T. T. Martin, of Blue Mountain, Miss., come to town with a truck-load of torches and hymn-books to put Darwin in his place. There was a singing brother bellowing apocalyptic hymns. There was William Jennings Bryan, followed everywhere by a gaping crowd. Dayton was having a roaring time. It was better than the circus. But the note of devotion was simply not there; the Daytonians, after listening a while, would slip away to Robinson's drug-store to regale themselves with coca-cola, or to the lobby of the Aqua Hotel, where the learned Raulston sat in state, judicially picking his teeth. The real religion was not present. It began at the bridge over the town creek, where the road makes off for the hills.

4

There is soft, gentle satire and there is satire that bites and stings. H. L. Mencken was a practitioner of the latter variety. While his comic depiction of a wedding as third-rate theater is not specifically concerned with the religious implications of matrimonial foolishness, any person who has agonized over the proper place of weddings in the church will come to the end of this piece thinking—sad but true. Have weddings changed for the better since Mencken wrote this in the early 1900s?

"THE WEDDING. A STAGE DIRECTION"*

H. L. Mencken

The scene is a church in an American city of about half a million population, and the time is about eleven o'clock of a fine morning in early spring. The neighborhood is well-to-do, but not quite fashionable. That is to say, most of the families of the vicinage keep two servants (alas, more or less intermittently!), and eat dinner at half-past six, and about one in every four boasts a colored butler (who attends to the fires, washes windows and helps with the sweeping), and a last year's automobile. The heads of these families are merchandise brokers; jobbers in notions, hardware and drugs; manufacturers of candy, hats, badges, office furniture, blank books, picture frames, wire goods and patent medicines; managers of steamboat lines; district agents of insurance companies; owners of commercial printing offices, and other such

*From *A Book of Burlesques*, by H. L. Mencken. Copyright 1916 by Alfred A. Knopf, Inc., and renewed 1944 by H. L. Mencken. Reprinted by permission of the publisher.

business men of substance—and the prosperous lawyers and popular family doctors who keep them out of trouble. In one block live a Congressman and two college professors, one of whom has written an unimportant textbook and got himself into "Who's Who in America." In the block above lives a man who once ran for Mayor of the city, and came near being elected.

The wives of these householders wear good clothes and have a liking for a reasonable gayety, but very few of them can pretend to what is vaguely called social standing, and, to do them justice, not many of them waste any time lamenting it. They have, taking one with another, about three children apiece, and are good mothers. A few of them belong to women's clubs or flirt with the suffragettes, but the majority can get all of the intellectual stimulation they crave in the Ladies' Home Journal and the Saturday Evening Post, with Vogue added for its fashions. Most of them, deep down in their hearts, suspect their husbands of secret frivolity, and about ten per cent. have the proofs, but it is rare for them to make rows about it, and the divorce rate among them is thus very low. Themselves indifferent cooks, they are unable to teach their servants the art, and so the food they set before their husbands and children is often such as would make a Frenchman cut his throat. But they are diligent housewives otherwise; they see to it that the windows are washed, that no one tracks mud into the hall, that the servants do not waste coal, sugar, soap and gas, and that the family buttons are always sewed on. In religion these estimable wives are pious in habit but somewhat nebulous in faith. That is to say, they regard any person who specifically refuses to go to church as a heathen, but they themselves are by no means regular in attendance, and not one in ten of them could tell you whether transubstantiation is a Roman Catholic or a Dunkard doctrine. About two per cent. have dallied more or less gingerly with Christian Science, their average period of belief being one year.

The church we are in is like the neighborhood and its people: well-to-do but not fashionable. It is Protestant in faith and probably Episcopalian. The pews are of thick, yellow-brown oak, severe in pattern and hideous in color. In each there is a long, removable cushion of a dark, purplish, dirty hue, with here and there some of its hair stuffing showing. The stained-glass windows, which were all bought ready-made and depict scenes from the New Testament, commemorate the virtues of departed worthies of the neighborhood, whose names appear, in illegible black letters, in the lower panels. The floor is covered with a carpet of some tough, fibrous material, apparently a sort of grass, and along the center aisle it is much worn. The normal smell of the place is rather less unpleasant than that of most other halls, for on the one day when it is regularly crowded practically all of the persons gathered together have been very recently bathed.

On this fine morning, however, it is full of heavy, mortuary perfumes, for a couple of florist's men have just finished decorating the chancel with flowers and potted palms. Just behind the chancel rail, facing the center aisle, there is a prie-dieu, and to either side of it are great banks of lilies, carnations, gardenias and roses. Three or four feet behind the prie-dieu and completely concealing the high altar, there is a dense jungle of palms. Those in the front rank are authentically growing in pots, but behind them the florist's men have artfully placed some more durable, and hence more profitable, sophistications. Anon the rev. clergyman, emerging from the vestry-room to the right, will pass along the front of this jungle to the prie-dieu, and so, framed in flowers, face the congregation with his saponaceous smile.

The florist's men, having completed their labors, are preparing to depart. The older of the two, a man in the fifties, shows the ease of an experienced hand by taking out a large plug of tobacco and gnawing off a substantial chew. The desire to spit seizing him shortly, he proceeds to gratify it by a trick long practised by gasfitters, musicians, caterer's helpers, piano movers and other such alien invaders of the domestic hearth. That is to say, he hunts for a place where the carpet is loose along the chancel rail, finds it where two lengths join, deftly turns up a flap, spits upon the bare floor, and then lets the flap fall back, finally giving it a pat with the sole of his foot. This done, he and his assistant leave the church to the sexton, who has been sweeping the vestibule, and, after passing the time of day with the two men who are putting up a striped awning from the door to the curb, disappear into a nearby speak-easy, there to wait and refresh themselves until the wedding is over, and it is time to take away their lilies, their carnations and their synthetic palms.

It is now a quarter past eleven, and two flappers of the neighborhood, giggling and arm-in-arm, approach the sexton and inquire of him if they may enter. He asks them if they have tickets and when they say they haven't, he tells them that he ain't got no right to let them in, and don't know nothing about what the rule is going to be. At some weddings, he goes on, hardly nobody ain't allowed in, but then again, sometimes they don't scarcely look at the tickets at all. *The two flappers retire abashed, and as the sexton finishes his sweeping, there enters the organist.*

The organist is a tall, thin man of melancholy, uremic aspect, wearing a black slouch hat with a wide brim and a yellow overcoat that barely reaches to his knees. A pupil, in his youth, of a man who had once studied (irregularly and briefly) with Charles-Marie Widor, he acquired thereby the artistic temperament and with it a vast fondness for malt liquor. His mood this morning is acidulous and depressed, for he spent yesterday evening in a Pilsner ausschank with two former members of the Boston Symphony Orchestra, and it was 3 A.M. before they finally agreed that Johann Sebastian Bach, all things considered, was a greater man than Beethoven, and so parted amicably. Sourness is the precise sensation that wells within him. He feels vinegary; his blood runs cold; he wishes he could immerse himself in bicarbonate of soda. But the call of his art is more potent than the protest of his poisoned and quaking liver, and so he manfully climbs the spiral stairway to his organ-loft.

Once there, he takes off his hat and overcoat, stoops down to blow the dust off the organ keys, throws the electrical switch which sets the bellows going, and then proceeds to take off his shoes. This done, he takes his seat, reaches for the pedals with his stockinged feet, tries an experimental 32-foot CCC, and then wanders gently into a Bach toccata. It is his limbering-up piece: he always plays it as a prelude to a wedding job. It thus goes very smoothly and even brilliantly, but when he comes to the end of it and tackles the ensuing fugue he is quickly in difficulties, and after four or five stumbling repetitions of the subject he hurriedly improvises a crude coda and has done. Peering down into the church to see if his flounderings have had an audience, he sees two old maids enter, the one very tall and thin and the other somewhat brisk and bunchy.

They constitute the vanguard of the nuptial throng, and as they proceed hesitatingly up the center aisle, eager for good seats but afraid to go too far, the organist wipes his palms upon his trousers legs, squares his shoulders, and plunges into the program that he has played at all weddings for fifteen years past. It begins with Mendelssohn's Spring Song, pianissimo. Then comes Rubinstein's Melody in F, with a touch of forte toward the close, and then Nevin's "Oh, That We Two Were

Maying," and then the Chopin waltz in A flat, Opus 69, No. 1, and then the Spring Song again, and then a free fantasia upon "The Rosary" and then a Moszkowski mazurka, and then the Dvorák Humoresque (with its heart-rending cry in the middle), and then some vague and turbulent thing (apparently the disjecta membra of another fugue), and then Tschaikowsky's "Autumn," and then Elgar's "Salut d'Amour," and then the Spring Song a third time, and then something or other from one of the Peer Gynt suites, and then an hurrah or two from the Hallelujah chorus, and then Chopin again, and Nevin, and Elgar, and—

But meanwhile, there is a growing activity below. First comes a closed automobile bearing the six ushers and soon after it another automobile bearing the bridegroom and his best man. The bridegroom and the best man disembark before the side entrance of the church and make their way into the vestry room, where they remove their hats and coats, and proceed to struggle with their cravats and collars before a mirror which hangs on the wall. The room is very dingy. A baize-covered table is in the center of it, and around the table stand six or eight chairs of assorted designs. One wall is completely covered by a bookcase, through the glass doors of which one may discern piles of cheap Bibles, hymn-books and back numbers of the parish magazine. In one corner is a small washstand. The best man takes a flat flask of whiskey from his pocket, looks about him for a glass, finds it on the washstand, rinses it at the tap, fills it with a policeman's drink, and hands it to the bridegroom. The latter downs it at a gulp. Then the best man pours out one for himself.

The ushers, reaching the vestibule of the church, have handed their silk hats to the sexton, and entered the sacred edifice. There was a rehearsal of the wedding last night, but after it was over the bride ordered certain incomprehensible changes in the plan, and the ushers are now completely at sea. All they know clearly is that the relatives of the bride are to be seated on one side and the relatives of the bridegroom on the other. But which side for one and which for the other? They discuss it heatedly for three minutes and then find that they stand three for putting the bride's relatives on the left side and three for putting them on the right side. The debate, though instructive, is interrupted by the sudden entrance of seven women in a group. They are headed by a *truculent old battleship, possibly an aunt or something of the sort, who fixes the nearest usher with a knowing, suspicious glance, and motions to him to show her the way.*

He offers her his right arm and they start up the center aisle, with the six other women following in irregular order, and the five other ushers scattered among the women. The leading usher is tortured damnably by doubts as to where the party should go. If they are aunts, to which house do they belong, and on which side are the members of that house to be seated? What if they are not aunts, but merely neighbors? Or perhaps an association of former cooks, parlor maids, nurse girls? Or strangers? The sufferings of the usher are relieved by the battleship, who halts majestically about twenty feet from the altar, and motions her followers into a pew to the left. They file in silently and she seats herself next the aisle. All seven settle back and wriggle for room. It is a tight fit.

(Who, in point of fact, are these ladies? Don't ask the question! The ushers never find out. No one ever finds out. They remain a joint mystery for all time. In the end they become a sort of tradition, and years hence, when two of the ushers meet, they will cackle over old dreadnaught and her six cruisers. The bride, grown old and fat, will tell the tale to her daughter, and then to her granddaughter. It will grow more and more strange, marvelous, incredible. Variorum versions will spring up. It will be adapted to other weddings. The dreadnaught will become an apparition, a witch, the Devil in skirts. And as the years pass, the date of the episode will be pushed back. By 2017 it will be dated 1150. By 2475 it will take on a sort of sacred character, and there will be a footnote referring to it in the latest Revised Version of the New Testament.)

It is now a quarter to twelve, and all of a sudden the vestibule fills with wedding guests. Nine-tenths of them, perhaps even nineteen-twentieths, are women, and most of them are beyond thirty-five. Scattered among them, hanging onto their skirts, are about a dozen little girls—one of them a youngster of eight or thereabout, with spindle shanks and shining morning face, entranced by her first wedding. Here and there lurks a man. Usually he wears a hurried, unwilling, protesting look. He has been dragged from his office on a busy morning, forced to rush home and get into his cutaway coat, and then marched to the church by his wife. One of these men, much hustled, has forgotten to have his shoes shined. He is intensely conscious of them, and tries to hide them behind his wife's skirt as they walk up the aisle. Accidentally he steps upon it, and gets a look over the shoulder which lifts his diaphragm an inch and turns his liver to water. This man will be courtmartialed when he reaches home, and he knows it. He wishes that some foreign power would invade the United States and burn down all the churches in the country, and that the bride, the bridegroom and all the other persons interested in the present wedding were dead and in hell.

The ushers do their best to seat these wedding guests in some sort of order, but after a few minutes the crowd at the doors becomes so large that they have to give it up, and thereafter all they can do is to hold out their right arms ingratiatingly and trust to luck. One of them steps on a fat woman's skirt, tearing it very badly, and she has to be helped back to the vestibule. There she seeks refuge in a corner, under a stairway leading up to the steeple, and essays to repair the damage with pins produced from various nooks and crevices of her person. Meanwhile the guilty usher stands in front of her, mumbling apologies and trying to look helpful. When she finishes her work and emerges from her improvised drydock, he again offers her his arm, but she sweeps past him without noticing him, and proceeds grandly to a seat far forward. She is a cousin to the bride's mother, and will make a report to every branch of the family that all six ushers disgraced the ceremony by appearing at it far gone in liquor.

Fifteen minutes are consumed by such episodes and divertisements. By the time the clock in the steeple strikes twelve the church is well filled. The music of the organist, who has now reached Mendelssohn's Spring Song for the third and last time, is accompanied by a huge buzz of whispers, and there is much craning of necks and long-distance nodding and smiling. Here and there an unusually gorgeous hat is the target of many converging glances, and of as many more or less satirical criticisms. To the damp funeral smell of the flowers at the altar, there has been added the cacodorous scents of forty or fifty different brands of talcum and rice powder. It begins to grow warm in the church, and a number of women open their vanity bags and duck down for stealthy dabs at their noses. Others, more reverent, suffer the agony of augmenting shines. One, a trickster, has concealed powder in her pocket handkerchief, and applies it dexterously while pretending to blow her nose.

The bridegroom in the vestry-room, entering upon the second year (or is it the third?) of his long and ghastly wait, grows increasingly nervous, and when he hears the organist pass from the Spring Song into some more sonorous and stately thing he mistakes it for the wedding march from "Lohengrin," and is hot for marching upon the altar at once. The best man, an old hand, restrains him gently, and administers another sedative from the bottle. The bridegroom's thoughts turn to gloomy things. He remembers sadly that he will never be able to laugh at benedicts again; that his days of low, rabelaisian wit and care-free scoffing are over; that he is now the very thing he mocked so gaily but yesteryear. Like a drowning man, he passes his whole life in review—not, however, that part which is past, but that part which is to come. Odd fancies throng upon him. He wonders what his honeymoon will cost him, what there will be to drink at the wedding breakfast, what a certain girl in Chicago will say when she hears of his marriage. Will there be any children? He rather hopes not, for all those he knows appear so greasy and noisy, but he decides that he might conceivably compromise on a boy. But how is he going to make sure that it will not be a girl? The thing, as yet, is a medical impossibility—but medicine is making rapid strides. Why not wait until the secret is discovered? This sapient compromise pleases the bridegroom, and he proceeds to a consideration of various problems of finance. And then, of a sudden, the organist swings unmistakably into "Lohengrin" and the best man grabs him by the arm.

There is now great excitement in the church. The bride's mother, two sisters, three brothers and three sisters-in-law have just marched up the center aisle and taken seats in the front pew, and all the women in the place are craning their necks toward the door. The usual electrical delay ensues. There is something the matter with the bride's train, and the two bridesmaids have a deuce of a time fixing it. Meanwhile the bride's father, in tight pantaloons and tighter gloves, fidgets and fumes in the vestibule, the six ushers crowd about him inanely, and the sexton rushes to and fro like a rat in a trap. Finally, all being ready, with the ushers formed two abreast, the sexton pushes a button, a small buzzer sounds in the organ loft, and the organist, as has been said, plunges magnificently into the fanfare of the "Lohengrin" march. Simultaneously the sexton opens the door at the bottom of the main aisle, and the wedding procession gets under weigh.

The bride and her father march first. Their step is so slow (about one beat to two measures) that the father has some difficulty in maintaining his equilibrium, but the bride herself moves steadily and erectly, almost seeming to float. Her face is thickly encrusted with talcum in its various forms, so that she is almost a dead white. She keeps her eyelids lowered modestly, but is still acutely aware of every glance fastened upon her—not in the mass, but every glance individually. For example, she sees clearly, even through her eyelids, the still, cold smile of a girl in Pew 8 R—a girl who once made an unwomanly attempt upon the bridegroom's affections, and was routed and put to flight by superior strategy. And her ears are open, too: she hears every "How sweet!" and "Oh, lovely!" and "Ain't she pale!" from the latitude of the last pew to the very glacis of the altar of God.

While she has thus made her progress up the hymeneal chute, the bridegroom and his best man have emerged from the vestryroom and begun the short march to the prie-dieu. They walk haltingly, clumsily, uncertainly, stealing occasional glances at the advancing bridal party. The bridegroom feels of his lower right-hand waistcoat pocket; the ring is still there. The best man wriggles his cuffs. No one, however, pays any heed to them. They are not even seen, indeed, until the bride and her father reach the open space in front of the altar. There the bride and the bridegroom find themselves standing side by side, but not a word is exchanged between them, nor even a look of recognition. They stand motionless, contemplating the ornate cushion at their feet, until the bride's father and the bridesmaids file to the left of the bride and the ushers, now wholly disorganized and imbecile, drape themselves in an irregular file along the altar rail. Then, the music having died down to a faint murmur and a hush having fallen upon the assemblage, they look up.

Before them, framed by foliage, stands the reverent gentleman of God who will presently link them in indissoluble chains—the estimable rector of the parish. He has got there just in time; it was, indeed, a close shave. But no trace of haste or of anything else of a disturbing character is now visible upon his smooth, glistening, somewhat feverish face. That face is wholly occupied by his official smile, a thing of oil and honey all compact, a balmy, unctuous illumination—the secret of his success in life. Slowly his cheeks puff out, gleaming like soap bubbles. Slowly he *lifts his prayer-book from the prie-dieu and holds it droopingly. Slowly his soft caressing eyes engage it. There is an almost imperceptible stiffening of his frame. His mouth opens with a faint click. He begins to read.*

The Ceremony of Marriage has begun.

5

Canadian-American humorist Stephen Leacock kept readers laughing for nearly half a century. His nonsense novels, burlesque dramas, and comic portraits are irresistibly funny. Leacock's portrait of the unfortunate Reverend Melpomenus Jones, while not specifically concerned with religion or the clergy, is an image of the compliant, desperate-to-please pastor who simply can't offend by saying good-bye. It stands as a warning to clergy that there are worse fates for a pastor than to be considered rude.

"THE AWFUL FATE OF MELPOMENUS JONES"*

Stephen Leacock

Some people—not you nor I, because we are so awfully self-possessed—but some people, find great difficulty in saying good-bye when making a call or spending the evening. As the moment draws near when the visitor feels that he is fairly entitled to go away he rises and says abruptly, "Well, I think I . . ." Then the people say, "Oh, must you go now? Surely it's early yet!" and a pitiful struggle ensues.

I think the saddest case of this kind of thing that I ever knew was that of my poor friend Melpomenus Jones, a curate—such a dear young man, and only twenty-three! He simply couldn't get away from people. He was too modest to tell a lie, and too religious to wish to appear rude. Now it happened that he went

*Reprinted by permission of the Bodley Head Ltd. from *The Bodley Head Leacock*, edited and introduced by J. B. Priestly.

to call on some friends of his on the very first afternoon of his summer vacation. The next six weeks were entirely his own—absolutely nothing to do. He chatted awhile, drank two cups of tea, then braced himself for the effort and said suddenly:

"Well, I think I . . ."

But the lady of the house said, "Oh, no! Mr. Jones, can't you really stay a little longer?"

Jones was always truthful. "Oh, yes," he said, "of course, I—er—can stay."

"Then please don't go."

He stayed. He drank eleven cups of tea. Night was falling. He rose again.

"Well, now," he said shyly, "I think I really . . ."

"You must go?" said the lady politely. "I thought perhaps you could have stayed to dinner . . ."

"Oh, well, so I could, you know," Jones said, "if . . ."

"Then please stay, I'm sure my husband will be delighted."

"All right," he said feebly. "I'll stay," and he sank back into his chair, just full of tea, and miserable.

Papa came home. They had dinner. All through the meal Jones sat planning to leave at eight-thirty. All the family wondered whether Mr. Jones was stupid and sulky, or only stupid.

After dinner mamma undertook to "draw him out," and showed him photographs. She showed him all the family museum, several gross of them—photos of papa's uncle and his wife, and mamma's brother and his little boy, an awfully interesting photo of papa's uncle's friend in his Bengal uniform, an awfully well-taken photo of papa's grandfather's partner's dog, and an awfully wicked one of papa as the devil for a fancy-dress ball.

At eight-thirty Jones had examined seventy-one photographs. There were about sixty-nine more that he hadn't. Jones rose.

"I must say good night now," he pleaded.

"Say good night!" they said, "why, it's only half-past eight! Have you anything to do?"

"Nothing," he admitted, and muttered something about staying six weeks, and then laughed miserably.

Just then it turned out that the favourite child of the family, such a dear little romp, had hidden Mr. Jones's hat; so Papa said that he must stay, and invited him to a pipe and a chat. Papa had the pipe and gave Jones the chat, and still he stayed. Every moment he meant to take the plunge, but couldn't. Then papa began to get very tired of Jones, and fidgeted and finally said, with jocular irony, that Jones had better stay all night, they could give him a shakedown. Jones mistook his meaning and thanked him with tears in his eyes, and papa put Jones to bed in the spare room and cursed him heartily.

After breakfast next day, papa went off to his work in the City, and left Jones playing with the baby, broken-hearted. His nerve was utterly gone. He was meaning to leave all day, but the thing had got on his mind and he simply couldn't. When papa came home in the evening he was surprised and chagrined to find Jones still there. He thought to jockey him out with a jest, and said he thought he'd have to charge him for his board, he! he! The unhappy young man stared wildly for a moment, then wrung papa's hand, paid him a month's board in advance, and broke down and sobbed like a child.

In the days that followed he was moody and unapproachable. He lived, of course, entirely in the drawing-room, and the lack of air and exercise began to tell sadly on his health. He passed his time in drinking tea and looking at the photographs. He would stand for hours gazing at the photographs of papa's uncle's friend in his Bengal uniform—talking to it, sometimes swearing bitterly at it. His mind was visibly failing.

At length, the crash came. They carried him upstairs in a raging delirium of fever. The illness that followed was terrible. He recognized no one, not even papa's uncle's friend in his Bengal uniform. At times he would start up from his bed and shriek, "Well, I think I . . ." and then fall back upon the pillow with a horrible laugh. Then, again, he would leap up and cry, "Another cup of tea and more photographs! More photographs! Har! Har!"

At length, after a month of agony, on the last day of his vacation, he passed away. They say that when the last moment came, he sat up in bed with a beautiful smile of confidence playing upon his face, and said, "Well—the angels are calling me; I'm afraid I really must go now. Good afternoon."

And the rushing of his spirit from its prison-house was as rapid as a hunted cat passing over a garden fence.

6

Journalist, author, and playwright George Ade captured the spirit of America at the turn of the century. He is best known for his fables in slang. In this piece, Ade pokes gentle fun at the mysterious world of church finance.

"THE FABLE OF THE GOOD PEOPLE WHO RALLIED TO THE SUPPORT OF THE CHURCH"*

George Ade

A Congregation needed Money for repairing the Church, so the Women got together and decided to hold a Raspberry Festival. Sister Frisbie invited them to come and Carouse on her Front Lawn. Some 22 Members of the Flock flew out and brought a few Things to Wear, the Outlay for washable Finery running to about $8 per Head.

Mr. Frisbie got $9 worth of Chinese Lanterns and strung them around. He wanted to do the Thing up Brown so as to get a Puff in the Weekly. The Paper came out and said that the Frisbie Front Yard with its Myriad Twinkling Lights was a Veritable Fairy-Land. That kind of a Notice is worth $9 of anybody's Money.

Mr. Frisbie and three other Pillars of the Church devoted $7 worth of valuable Time to unloading Tables and Campstools.

The Women Folks ruined $14 worth of Complexion working in the hot Kitchen to make Angel Food and Fig Cake.

On the Night of the Raspberry Orgy the Public Trampled down $45 worth of Shrubbery.

*From *The America of George Ade*.

45

When it came time to check up the Linen and Silverware it was found that $17 worth of Spoons with Blue Thread tied around them had been lost in the Shuffle.

The Drip from the Candles ruined $29 worth of Summer Suits and Percale Shirt-Waists.

Four Children gorged themselves and each was tied in a True Lover's Knot with Cholera Morbus before another Sunrise. The Doctor Bills footed up $18.

After clearing the Wreck, paying the Drayman and settling for the Ice Cream and Berries, it was discovered that the Church was $6.80 to the Good. So everybody said it was a Grand Success.

Moral: *Anything to avoid dropping it in the Basket.*

7

Sometimes the humorist enables us to laugh to keep from crying. For years, Jewish humorist Harry Golden skillfully used laughter as a weapon against bigotry and injustice. Founder and publisher of The Carolina Israelite *newspaper, Golden angered Southerners who fought to maintain the structures of racism in the South but he gave a hopeful smile to those who were trying to bring about change.*

"The Vertical Negro Plan" is Golden's most famous piece. It appeared in response to the 1954 Brown vs. The Board of Education of Topeka *decision which called for the desegregation of public facilities in the United States. Golden noted the ironies within southern segregationist laws. Since the legislature had declared it legal for blacks and whites to gather in public buildings as long as they did not sit together, Golden proposed eliminating all chairs in the schools—standing intergration. Since black people could only attend white movie theaters if they were accompanying white children, he proposed the "White Baby Plan" whereby blacks could borrow white children when they wanted to attend the theater.*

"The Vertical Negro Plan," while not specifically about religion or the church, is a classic example of how humor undercuts injustice.

"THE VERTICAL NEGRO PLAN"*

Harry Golden

Those who love North Carolina will jump at the chance to share in the great responsibility confronting our governor and the State Legislature. A special session of the Legislature (July 25-28, 1956) passed a series of amendments to the State

---

*From *Only in America*. Used by permission of Amereon Ltd.

Constitution. These proposals submitted by the Governor and his Advisory Education Committee included the following:

(A) The elimination of the compulsory attendance law, "to prevent any child from being forced to attend a school with a child of another race."

(B) The establishment of "Education Expense Grants" for education in a private school, "in the case of a child assigned to a public school attended by a child of another race."

(C) A "uniform system of local option" whereby a majority of the folks in a school district may suspend or close a school if the situation becomes "intolerable."

But suppose a Negro child applies for this "Education Expense Grant" and says he wants to go to the private school too? There are fourteen Supreme Court decisions involving the use of public funds; there are only two "decisions" involving the elimination of racial discrimination in the public schools.

The Governor has said that critics of these proposals have not offered any constructive advice or alternatives. Permit me, therefore, to offer an idea for the consideration of the members of the regular sessions. A careful study of my plan, I believe, will show that it will save millions of dollars in tax funds and eliminate forever the danger to our public education system. Before I outline my plan, I would like to give you a little background.

One of the factors involved in our tremendous industrial growth and economic prosperity is the fact that the South, voluntarily, has all but eliminated VERTICAL SEGREGATION. The tremendous buying power of the twelve million Negroes in the South has been based wholly on the absence of racial segregation. The white and Negro stand at the same grocery and supermarket counters; deposit money at the same bank teller's window; pay phone and light bills to the same clerk; walk through the same dime and department stores, and stand at the same drugstore counters.

It is only when the Negro "sets" that the fur begins to fly.

Now, since we are not even thinking about restoring VERTICAL SEGREGATION, I think my plan would not only comply with the Supreme Court decisions, but would maintain "sitting-down" segregation. Now here is the GOLDEN VERTICAL NEGRO PLAN. Instead of all those complicated proposals, all the next session needs to do is pass one small amendment which would provide *only* desks in all the public schools of our state—*no seats*.

The desks should be those standing-up jobs, like the old-fashioned bookkeeping desk. Since no one in the South pays the slightest attention to a VERTICAL NEGRO, this will completely solve our problem. And it is not such a terrible inconvenience for young people to stand up during their classroom studies. In fact, this may be a blessing in disguise. They are not learning to read sitting down, anyway; maybe standing up will help. This will save more millions of dollars in the cost of our remedial English course when the kids enter college. In whatever direction you look with the GOLDEN VERTICAL NEGRO PLAN, you save millions of dollars, to say nothing of eliminating forever any danger to our public education system upon which rests the destiny, hopes, and happiness of this society.

My WHITE BABY PLAN offers another possible solution to the segregation problem—this time in a field other than education.

Here is an actual case history of the "White Baby Plan To End Racial Segregation":

Some months ago there was a revival of the Laurence Olivier movie, *Hamlet*, and several Negro schoolteachers were eager to see it. One Saturday afternoon they asked some white friends to lend them two of their little children, a three-year-old girl and a six-year-old boy, and, holding these white children by the hands, they obtained tickets from the movie-house cashier without a moment's hesitation. They were in like Flynn.

This would also solve the baby-sitting problem for thousands and thousands of white working mothers. There can be a mutual exchange of references, then the people can sort of pool their children at a central point in each neighborhood, and every time a Negro wants to go to the movies all she needs to do is pick up a white child—and go.

Eventually the Negro community can set up a factory and manufacture white babies made of plastic, and when they want to go to the opera or to a concert, all they need do is carry that plastic doll in their arms. The dolls, of course, should all have blond curls and blue eyes, which would go even further; it would give the Negro woman and her husband priority over the whites for the very best seats in the house.

While I still have faith in the WHITE BABY PLAN, my final proposal may prove to be the most practical of all.

Only after a successful test was I ready to announce formally the GOLDEN "OUT-OF-ORDER" PLAN.

I tried my plan in a city of North Carolina, where the Negroes represent 39 per cent of the population.

I prevailed upon the manager of a department store to shut the water off in his "white" water fountain and put up a sign, "Out-of-Order." For the first day or two the whites were hesitant, but little by little they began to drink out of the water fountain belonging to the "coloreds"—and by the end of the third week everybody was drinking the "segregated" water; with not a single solitary complaint to date.

I believe the test is of such sociological significance that the Governor should appoint a special committee of two members of the House and two Senators to investigate the GOLDEN "OUT-OF-ORDER" PLAN. We kept daily reports on the use of the unsegregated water fountain which should be of great value to this committee. This may be the answer to the necessary uplifting of the white morale. It is possible that the whites may accept desegregation if they are assured that the facilities are still "separate," albeit "Out-of-Order."

As I see it now, the key to my Plan is to keep the "Out-of-Order" sign up for at least two years. We must do this thing gradually.

8

Even as the Reverend Elmer Gantry stands as the comic image of the conservative religious shyster, so the Reverend Andrew Mackerel (who prefers to be known simply as Mr. Mackerel) is the prototype of the liberal, avant-garde clerical fake. When not engaged in feverish romantic exploits among his female parishioners, Mackerel is attempting to distance himself from all traditional notions of ministerial behavior.

Mackerel is the creation of novelist Peter De Vries in The Mackerel Plaza. *Religion, serious and otherwise, is a frequent theme in the writing of De Vries. In this first selection from the book, Mackerel describes the distinctive architecture of his parish, People's Liberal—a church that embodies everything that could go wrong in modern, liberal Christianity.*

In the second selection, Mackerel appears before the local Town Council which is considering naming a plaza for Mackerel's late wife—a woman who met her demise at a church picnic under suspicious circumstances and who is not at all mourned by the philandering husband she left behind. Mackerel is determined to have a fight with the Council over some issue. When no issue is forthcoming, he does his best to create one. The result is the wickedly funny satire of Peter De Vries at its best.

PEOPLE'S LIBERAL CHURCH*

Peter De Vries

Our church is, I believe, the first split-level church in America. It has five rooms and two baths downstairs—dining

*From *The Mackerel Plaza* by Peter De Vries. Copyright © 1958, renewed 1986, by Peter De Vries. Original publication by Little, Brown & Company, Inc. Reprinted by permission of Watkins/Loomis, Inc.

area, kitchen and three parlors for committee and group meetings—with a crawl space behind the furnace ending in the hillside into which the structure is built. Upstairs is one huge all-purpose interior, divisible into different-sized components by means of sliding walls and convertible into an auditorium for putting on plays, a gymnasium for athletics, and a ballroom for dances. There is a small worship area at one end. This has a platform cantilevered on both sides, with a free-form pulpit designed by Noguchi. It consists of a slab of marble set on four legs of four delicately differing fruitwoods, to symbolize the four Gospels, and their failure to harmonize. Behind it dangles a large multicolored mobile, its interdenominational parts swaying, as one might fancy, in perpetual reminder of the Pauline stricture against those "blown by every wind of doctrine." Its proximity to the pulpit inspires a steady flow of more familiar congregational whim, at which we shall not long demur, going on with our tour to say that in back of this building is a newly erected clinic, with medical and neuropsychiatric wings, both indefinitely expandable. Thus People's Liberal is a church designed to meet the needs of today, and to serve the whole man. This includes the worship of a God free of outmoded theological definitions and palatable to a mind come of age in the era of Relativity. "It is the final proof of God's omnipotence that he need not exist in order to save us," Mackerel had preached. (I hope I may be indulged these shifts into the third person in relating things about which I am a trifle self-conscious.) At any rate, this aphorism seemed to his hearers so much better than anything Voltaire had said on the subject that he was given an immediate hike in pay and invited out to more dinners than he could possibly eat.

9

MACKEREL AT THE MEETING*

Peter De Vries

The council chamber is a room forty feet wide, in which the mayor and ten selectmen hold their official sessions. Mayor Junior was to have charge of proceedings tonight and already sat at the head of the long conference table in one of those black, high-backed leather swivel chairs, studded with buttons like navels, nursing a gavel. Strewn at his feet were members of the Chamber of Commerce and the businessmen interested in the Plaza, categories which greatly blended. Along one end of the room is a visitors' gallery with about forty or fifty seats. A handful of them were occupied by slouching spectators, who twitched tentatively when I strode in. Turnbull was among them, and likewise Comstock, covering the meeting for the *Globe*.

"Oh, Andy," said Mayor Junior, rising to shake my hand. "I guess you know everybody." I nodded crisply, declining his outslung arm, determined to have no soft soap but a clean fight. They would not embrace me in order to crush me. I sat down at the table behind a name plate which read "Melvin Pryzalski."

"I think we can make this brief and friendly," the mayor began. "My friend Andy here has taken exception—perfectly within his democratic right—to some aspects of the Plaza thing. We know what some of them are, but in case he has others, let's hear him out so we can whomp out a little agreement among us

*From *The Mackerel Plaza* by Peter De Vries. Copyright © 1958, renewed 1986, by Peter De Vries. Original publication by Little, Brown & Company, Inc. Reprinted by permission of Watkins/Loomis, Inc.

that will be satisfactory to all and leave no hard feelings with anybody. The main thing will be to separate the esplanade from the shopping center, to which I think we can all agree. However, if Andy—I'm sure he's that to all of us—has something further, why we can add that to the little agreement I've drawn up, sign it and get home in time to hear Ed Morrow, eh, fellows? He's got Gina Lollobrigida on tonight."

I saw what I was up against. The mayor was a numskull apparently without any sense of his role as a diehard reactionary. The smiles of the rest indicated a counciliatory attitude that also augured poorly for an open conflict, with battle lines clearly drawn and blood split where it must. "We'll do anything you want," Sponsible was saying, "within reason." Good Lord! Evidently I must instruct them in the rudiments of their own skulduggery if this thing was to be guided on classic lines, or anything like them. Very well, I would needle them into a proper assumption of their parts.

"Not so fast, boys," I said, rising. "Let's not muddle the issues with pretended sweetness and light. Society as it is constituted leaves no room for compromise with those playing the power game and those daring to say them nay. The struggle between them is total, and admits of only one result—a fight to the finish."

They exchanged baffled looks and bewildered shrugs. Their comprehension of the factors involved was more elementary than I had imagined. I must begin with the simplest fundamentals.

"Social elements thus in opposition," I continued, "enact dramatico-metaphoric embodiments of tribal drives which are at the same time religious in nature. When the economic interests of those in power—now get this—when they congeal with their emotional ones, we have the complete myth in a given culture. This myth operates on all levels and against all opposition, because that opposition challenges both the pocketbook and the prejudice. The Mackerel Plaza is an example of such a myth in our time and in our place because it satisfies all those requirements. It unites your material with your instinctual interests, and having embraced it as sacrosanct, you will defend it with every resource at your command."

"We will?" the mayor said, screwing his face up.

I nodded. "You will stop at nothing. It is an inevitable part of the power pattern." I paused. "Are there any more questions?"

The mayor looked around at his colleagues again for help. He was clearly out of his depth. A man on his right spoke up.

"But we just said we're perfectly willing to sit down with you and—"

"Ah, ah. Cards on the table, gentlemen, please. We dispense with token displays of amity and strike straight for the essentials. No mealy-mouthed equivocation and transparent subterfuge."

A man whom I recognized as Scanlon the paving contractor scratched his head.

"But, gee, we think you're a nice guy and . . ."

"It's no use. Compromise is impossible. It's you against me. One of us must go down in defeat. Already the fire crackles and the idol yawns, but I warn you, gentlemen. Truth crushed to earth will rise again, and blood of the martyrs is the seed of the church!"

The mayor crooked his finger at his neighbor and bent his head toward him. Others did the same, frowning in frank perplexity and whispering together. A thin man sitting all alone at the end of the table turned a pair of sad, chocolate eyes on me and said, "You don't have to bully us. We're only doing our best."

"I'm not trying to bully you," I said. "I'm only trying to bring to a head the inevitable. There's no point in wasting time in amenities that are doomed to failure. Let's have done with the politics and declare the war!"

He lowered his eyes meekly and resumed picking at a crack in the veneer of the table top. It was Kerfoot, the electrical engineer and lickspittle, who had been present at the luncheon where all this had been hatched. Others seemed equally cowed. Presently he turned to old Meesum on his right and some distance down the table. Meesum had been making circles on a pad with the expression of a man who resents being smoked out. Finally he droppd his pencil and leaned toward a group which included his mayor son. The buzz of voices rose till it was like a beehive.

Are you watching, Knopf? Are your getting all this? They have their heads together, and their voices as they speak are as the sound of knives being whetted, and as wind in savage grass.

"Are there any other questions?" I asked. "Before we get on with it?"

A stocky man in a gray suit got up. It was Sponsible, the head of the excavating firm. He was a self-made man in the sense that he had himself once driven the bulldozers now operated for him by others. He had just returned from a sunny two weeks in Florida, and his face looked like a burnt pan. There are people whose very appearance bespeaks their line of work, and there was about Hugh Sponsible's knobbed hands and his figure and even his voice a loose, hard, easy-rattling something that seemed to say we are not dust but gravel.

"You say we're supposed to railroad you on all them levels."

"That is correct."

"Just how do we go about doing this? Could you give us a few pointers?"

"Certainly. You will do it first through your ownership of the mass media: the press, radio and television, the mouths of old women. You will engage in attacks both on my intellectual position and my character. The latter has already begun. All this will be aimed toward your final coup—the attempted removal of my means of livelihood."

Sponsible nodded, stroking his nose, in perfect willingness to accept instruction in his role as oppressor but still retaining certain doubts to be aired.

"Can't we live and let live?"

"No. That is against your nature. Individually, yes; collectively, no. There your instinct is to protect the cash nexus of society, as Karl Marx has called it."

Sponsible sat down and a hand went up at the other end of the table.

"Yes?" I said. It was Scanlon again.

"I'm a simple man without much knowledge of these things, so I'll have to follow the leadership of others," he said. "But about this myth business. I don't quite get that. How we use that to make a buck and so on. Could you explain that a little more?"

"I'm glad you asked that question," I said. Now we were coming to grips. "I'll give you an example of how you're working it. The first thing you, the reigning oligarchy, do is popularize a utilizable figure, but in order to elevate it for the greatest number you vulgarize it. Just before coming here I read the announcement on the bulletin board about this wishing well twaddle." The mayor stirred in his chair and a small fidget ran along other parts of the table. "This is *real* mythology, boys."

"Why?" said the mayor.

"Why? Because Mrs. Mackerel had a mind like a steel trap, an antiseptic, sardonic, modern mind. One of often surgically cruel precision. She could never in all her born days have said a sappy, pappy, preposterous thing like that."

Wounded anger replaced the mayor's air of simple confusion.

"I don't understand what you mean," he said. "What's sappy about that story? I think it's nice."

"If you don't know, I can't explain it to you. Where did you hear such a thing?"

"Why, I found it in a publicity release. I . . . don't see our press agent here . . ."

"You see?" I shot at Sponsible. "Press agents making up little legends fit for mass consumption. And that 'effective tomorrow' bit. Who's gem was that?"

"Mine," said the mayor resentfully. "What's wrong with that? Doesn't every tradition have to get started *some*time?"

That's right," I said with a smile. "Ida May used to say, 'One dreams of the goddess Fame and winds up with the bitch Publicity.' "

A red-faced man I didn't know shook his finger across the table at me. "I don't think she used language like that and I don't think you ought to use it here!" he said.

"And calling her cruel," Scanlon said to him.

"That story illustrates a fine little sentiment and I think it's true."

The hubbub grew in volume, supported by exchanged nods. The gallery loungers were now galvanized into quite erect positions. Charlie Comstock's pencil galloped. Turnbull kneaded his mustache excitedly. As Junior banged his gavel I surveyed the scene with an inward smile. The caldron was boiling briskly. Who could doubt my thesis now?

Junior was rapping for silence for his old pa, who had signaled for the floor. They were all glad to see the old fox rise and take it: he would represent them well.

"This memorial is close to the heart of all of us," he began, laying his hand on his heart, where his wallet palpably bulged, "and I am so glad to hear Mr. Mackerel speak of putting the cards on the table. But let's do one more thing. *Let's turn them face up.*" He paused to let this sink in, greeting it himself with a burst of unrequited laughter. "Let's ask for his motives in all this. Let's ask whether he's opposed to just this bandwagon, this trough in which he says we've all got our snouts, or to *private profit as such.*"

Swell.

"I'm opposed to cracking open to commercial exploitation the last smidgen of scenic beauty left in this damned town. You got your way by befuddling a philanthropist into parting with more than he intended."

"Where shall we expand then, man!"

"What do I care?"

"Do you realize how dense the population of this town is?"

"I have inklings," I said, looking him steadily in the eye.

"You quoted Karl Marx. Are you a Communist?"

All gall is divided into three parts, I have thought since. First there is the basic glandular structure from which the trait derives its name; second, the nervous make-up and shadings of temperament which result in the gift of aggression; and lastly a certain density of mind which blinds the character to the resentment he inspires in others. Meesum had all these requirements in an unabridged degree, and that was why he struck everybody, and not just me, as the brassiest man they ever met. One or two, including Sprackling the young lawyer who had slipped in late, laughed. Most of them, even those whom I had goaded into a sense of their function as oppressors, looked to me to answer this absurd question with a loud negative.

I was not going to let them off so easy. I must lure them on to a full measure of accusation, to drive home to them the depth of their complicity in this enterprise. Guilt by association turned around. They must see that they were equally yoked with their spokesman in a cabal against me.

"Well, the early Christians were Communists, weren't they?" I answered evasively. (They didn't have anthing to share, but I must give Meesum enough rope.)

Meesum grasped his lapels firmly in both hands, and I remembered its having been said that he had once had ecclesiastical ambitions.

"Do you know how many sheep Abraham had?"

"Abraham who?"

"Abraham of old. How many cattle? How many acres of land? He was a very rich man."

"Not as a result of private initiative. I understand he got it all from God."

This was a barb that really went home. Nothing could more have incited Meesum, who had inherited everything he himself owned.

"I'm glad to hear you mention God," he said. "You do it little enough in church. You said once in a sermon that the common people must have loved gods, they made so many of them. Do you think that was respectful?"

"Of whom, Lincoln or God?"

Meesum raised and tightened his grip on his lapels, as though in his rage he had only himself to cling to for support. I suspected what was eating him especially these days. He had tried to settle the division, created in his mind by the conflicting genealogical societies as to his ancestry, by retaining a third, which claimed to have uncovered Moorish origins totally absent from the reports of the other two. This had unnerved him further and shortened his temper acutely.

"It is rumored that on Saturday nights you go about heckling street corner evangelists," he said. "Is that true?"

"I have often heckled them, yes."

"Is that conduct befitting a minister of the Gospel?"

"I feel it my duty to oppose vulgarity in any form. Such men are to religion what jingoism is to patriotism."

"Hear! hear!" shouted a voice in the gallery. It was a bull-necked man in a red mackinaw. "National sovereignty must go! Only world government will save us!"

Junior rapped him out of order, not, however, till he had let him finish his piece, to point up the type who might be expected to rally to my banner. Old Meesum improved the occasion by consulting some notes he had taken from his pocket. Evidently he had come prepared for this cross-questioning.

"You also once said—correct me if I misquote you— 'It is the final proof of God's omnipotence that he need not exist in order to save us.' " I acknowledged the accuracy of the quotation with a nod. "Doesn't that sound a lot like Voltaire?"

"Voltaire said something quite different. You're probably thinking of his aphorism, 'If there were no God, it would be necessary to invent him.' I go beyond that. I take the final step whereby theology, annihilating itself, sets religion free."

"Oh, you think you're smarter than Voltaire."

"Why, are you a fan of his?"

Meesum raised his cards above his head and slammed them down on the table. "I will not stand here and argue with a man who won't stick to the point!" he said, and sat down with almost as violent a contact with his chair as the cards had had with the table.

There was another silence. Mayor Junior looked miserably around. They looked at me with reproving, hangdog glances. The meeting seemed to have foundered. "Why didn't you bring all this up at the luncheon at the Stilton that time?" the mayor asked. "You were there."

"I didn't know at the time that it would take on this mythos-ethos opposition," I said. "How could I know that then?"

Sponsible raised his hand again and said a few words.

"Well, I just want to say that I appreciate Reverend Mackerel's objections. About the Plaza, the way it was gone at," he remarked. "But that's natural in a big enterprise. Mistakes will be made, excesses be guilty of. Sure it's a splash. Sure its ballyhoo. But why shouldn't we remember on as big a scale as possible somebody who gave herself on as big a scale as possible? After all, didn't she make the supreme sacrifice?"

He sat down to a round of applause and pats on the back. This was the moment, for me. He had stated the specific myth. It was up to me whether I was going to let it pass, or challenge it. Speak now or forever hold your peace. Are you ready, Prometheus?

I had an idea. Maybe I could get across by indirection what I had never been able to blurt out directly. Didn't I owe to Turnbull, even more than to them, this deliverance from the marshes of myth to the dry land of reality? I could put them one step from the truth, and let them take the last one by inference.

"Yes, I have always thought her deed a noble one," I said. "All the more so because she couldn't swim a stroke."

This was followed by a complete and absolute silence. In it, you could sense speculation like a foundless seething going on all around you. They seemed suspended in a vacuum for a moment. Then one of the heads turned slowly to Sprackling. Then another, then a third. They were making inference all right.

Sprackling rose. He had come really only to relinquish his legal duties for the Plaza, having just been appointed an assistant prosecuting attorney, and had not expected to participate on these lines.

"If the late Mrs. Mackerel couldn't swim," he said, "how was it you could run the risk of taking her out in a canoe?"

I followed the trajectory of this notion with a kind of dreamy detachment, turning my head in a looping glance to the left, as if in pursuit of an object describing an arc.

"Risk?" I said, driving the word through a bung in my throat.

"Yes. I should consider it so. Canoes tip over."

"Now you're doing it!" I told them. "Oppressing me. Now you're getting the hang of it. This is what I meant. Well might you ask, 'To what green altar, O mysterious priest, lead'st thou that heifer loving at the skies?' Might it not be, my lord, the altar of Mammon himself?"

"I should like to remind you that this is a serious hearing, despite its apparent informality, and not an exercise in this Machiavellian mumbo jumbo you seem to have on the brain," Sprackling said. "Now, I was asking you if it wasn't dangerous to go out in a canoe under the circumstances. They tip over."

"It never would have if she hadn't stood up and rocked it, which in turn wouldn't have happened if the crisis hadn't arisen that did. So from that point of view she did give her life for another, and the monument is in perfect order," I said. "Well then. Does that bring the questions to an end? If so, I think we can call it an evening and get on to Ed Murrow—"

"Not so fast," Sprackling said. "Aspects of this thing do arouse one's curiosity, which I hope you don't mind satisfying. Whose idea was it to go out in a canoe—rather than rent one of the numerous rowboats available?"

"Oh, hers. I was against it at first, my lord, but she won me over. We had quite an argument about it, but she won me over. She always won the arguments. Everything in order there, eh, my lord?"

I spoke, despite the witticism, with my head somewhat atilt and with that high assurance that distinguishes the true martyr from the sullen scapegoat. The vocative was a kind of arm offered to help them up a step onto this higher plane, too, while also supplying a dash of irony we all needed, a bit of garlic of parody rubbed on the strong meat of these proceedings.

"Did you and Mrs. Mackerel argue often? Quarrel bitterly, perhaps?"

I executed a series of gestures in the air in front of me, as though directing traffic of great size and complexity. "Happiness is no laughing matter, as the Irishman said."

At this point a minor disturbance broke out in the gallery. Some, including the internationalist who had been furtively distributing pamphlets on behalf of his own cause, began debating the propriety of this line of questioning, and their words became a free-for-all which also divided the committee around the table. "You have no right to ask him things like that here," one of my defenders called out, "Wait till you get him in court." The commotion subsided when Turnbull's tall figure rose in the front of the gallery. He asked for the floor and got it.

"I think it's time I spoke up here," he said. "Andy Mackerel is my friend and so was Ida May. I'm not as embarrassed by this as you might think. She deserves this memorial because of her life anyway, so the way she died doesn't make that much difference. But it does for Andrew's peace of mind and future welfare in this community. So we ought to go into the facts of that accident a little more fully for his sake, and settle them if we can. Now can anybody shed any light on it?"

In the silence their expressions asked him what he meant.

"I mean there must have been eye witnesses to the event. On that crowded beach. You were all *there*," he said, spreading his rangy arms. "You were all eye witnesses to the scene in general. But did anybody see that particular *part* of what happened in the cove?"

Another silence followed this query. It lasted fifteen seconds, half a minute. No one volunteered.

"I guess that's that then," Turnbull said. "Obviously *I* can't settle it. I was bobbing around on an inner tube."

A small figure rose behind him and spoke up in a high-pitched voice. It was young Shively, the druggist's son.

"I don't know if this'll be of any help," he said, "but there was somebody there who was taking pictures from the dock at the time. Movies, I mean. It was Waldo Hale. He had that movie camera of his along and started shooting when the motor launch got loose. That was all fun, of course, and he got some footage of it, but then the other happened. That was probably in it, so his mother said he hadn't oughta have the reel developed. In fact she wanted him to burn it, I remember. Whether he did or not, or ever got it developed, I can't say. I don't know."

Sprackling, who had momentarily sat down, rose again, fingering his Phi Beta Kappa key. "Is Waldo Hale here?" he asked.

"No," said the Shively youth, "and he ain't in town either. He's in the Army, Fort Bliss, down in Texas."

"Mrs. Hale?"

"His mother passed away last fall, sir. Neither of his parents is alive and the house is shut up. Waldo and I exchange letters once in a while, so maybe I could write to him and ask him about the film. I mean if I could be of any . . ."

"That won't be necessary," said Sprackling, hurriedly gathering up some papers and thrusting them into his briefcase. "We'll telephone Fort Bliss tonight."

10

Popular columnist for The Atlanta Constitution *and* The Atlanta Journal, *Lewis Grizzard has quickly become a foremost humorist of the contemporary American South. His bittersweet humor is exemplified by this selection which first recalls a preacher from his boyhood memory and then tells us about a pastoral visit before Grizzard's own open-heart surgery.*

"GOOD MEN OF GOD"*

Lewis Grizzard

Brother Dave Gardner, the southern philosopher, used to talk about how his mother had wanted him to be a man of God.

"My mother used to say, 'Son, you could make a million dollars preaching,' " he would begin. "I'd say, 'Yeah, Mama, but what the hell would I spend it on?' "

It's not easy being a preacher, especially these days. Preachers have to work harder than ever before keeping their flocks in line what with temptations at a new all-time high. I suppose the really big-time preachers, like Billy Graham and Oral Roberts and Jerry Falwell, have it made, though. Every time I pick up a newspaper there's a story about one of those heavyweight television preachers making a trip to Russia, or speaking out on international issues, or having a vision that tells him to go out and raise a few million bucks.

I always wonder when those guys find time to work on their

---

*Reprinted by permission of Peachtree Publishers, Ltd., from *They Tore Out My Heart and Stomped That Sucker Flat* by Lewis Grizzard. Copyright © 1982 by Lewis Grizzard.

sermons. When do they visit the sick and marry people and preach funerals?

Who mows the grass around their churches, and if one of their followers has a problem, like he lost his job and his wife split and his trailer burned all in the same week, when do those preachers have time to go talk to the poor soul?

I'm old-fashioned when it comes to preachers. I grew up in a small Methodist congregation, and I got used to preachers who were always there when you needed them, who mowed the grass around the church, and who even knocked down the dirt daubers' nests in the windows of the sanctuary so the dirt daubers wouldn't bother the worshippers while the preacher was trying to run the devil out of town on Sunday mornings. Every time I see Billy Graham on Meet the Press or catch Oral Roberts or Jerry Falwell on the tube, I always wonder if they have ever knocked down any dirt daubers' nests. Every time I see any of those high-powered evangelists, I also wonder whatever happened to Brother Roy Dodd Hembree, who tried but never quite made it over the hump into the land of evangelical milk and honey.

Brother Roy Dodd came to town every summer when I was a kid with his traveling tent revival and his two daughters, Nora and Cora. Nora was the better looking of the two, but Cora had more sense. Nora would do just about anything, including get bad drunk and then tell her daddy what local bird dog had bought her the beer. Brother Roy Dodd would then alert the sheriff's office in whatever county he happened to be preaching in at the time and demand the heathan buying Nora beer be locked up for the duration of his revival as a means of protecting his daughters.

Neither Nora nor Cora needed much protection, if the truth be known. Nora could cuss her way out of most any tight spot, and Cora had a black belt in switchblade.

Brother Roy Dodd's tent revival was the highlight of our summer, not only because of the opportunities Nora and Cora afforded, but also because Brother Roy Dodd put on a show that was in thrills and sheer excitement second only to the geek who bit the heads off live chickens at the county fair each fall.

They said Brother Roy Dodd was from over in Alabama and he used to be a Triple-A country singer until he got messed up with a woman one night in a beer joint where he was singing. The woman did a lot of winking and lip-pooching at Brother Roy Dodd during his act, and later, she told him her husband had gone to Shreveport to pick up a load of chickens and wouldn't be home until Saturday morning and there was still an hour or so left in Thursday.

Brother Roy Dodd, they said, knew there was trouble when, as he and the woman were in the midst of celebrating Friday night, he detected a poultry-like odor about the room. That was just before he heard two gunshots. Brother Roy Dodd caught one in each hip and it was shortly after the shooting, he found the Lord.

When he had recovered from his injuries, Brother Roy Dodd bought a tent and an old school bus and set out to spread the Word and his interpretation of it with a Bible he borrowed from his hospital room.

One night in Palatka, Florida, Brother Roy Dodd converted fourteen, including a young woman who had done some winking and lip-pooching of her own during the service.

After the service, Brother Roy Dodd confirmed the fact his winking and lip-pooching convert had no husband nor any connection with the business of transporting chickens, and asked the young woman if she would like to leave Palatka behind her. She consented and they said Brother Roy Dodd married himself to her, standing right there in the sawdust.

Her name was Dora. Hence, Nora and Cora. Dora learned to play piano and accompany Brother Roy Dodd when he sang the hymn of invitation each night, "Just As I Am (Without One Plea)," but Nora and Cora strayed early. Nora was smoking when she was nine, drinking when she was eleven, and she ran off one night with a sawmill hand from Boaz, Alabama, when she was thirteen, but came back three weeks later, with his truck and the $50 he gave her to leave.

Cora was a couple of years younger than Nora and they said

she had taken after her daddy as far as music went, but she had a wild side, too, and learned how to knife fight the year she spent in reform school when she was fourteen. Her crime was lifting the wallet out of a deputy sheriff's trousers, the pair he shouldn't have taken off in the back seat of his cruiser out behind the tent one night during a revival near Swainsboro, Georgia.

My older cousin took me to see Brother Roy Dodd the first time. I was nine. My cousin was sixteen and he had a car. Everybody else came to find the Lord. My cousin came to find Nora and Cora, which he did. I said I could find a ride home, and the next day, he told me how Nora had taken drunk later that night and how Cora had tried to cut a man for looking at her wrong.

"I never heard such cussing as Nora did," my cousin said.

"You ought to have heard her daddy," I said.

I had never heard anybody speak in tongues before I heard Brother Roy Dodd. He was up front of everybody and he was rolling forth out of Galatians, when, suddenly, he was caught in the spirit.

He eyes rolled back in his head and his voice boomed out through the tent:

"ALIDEEDOO! ALUDEEDOO! BOOLEYBOOLEY-BOOLEY-BOO!"

"Praise God, he's in the spirit!" said a woman behind me.

"Praise God, he is!" said her husband.

"Don't reckon Brother Roy Dodd's sick, do you?" asked another man, obviously a first-timer.

Brother Roy Dodd tongue-spoke for a good six or eight minutes before the spirit finally left him and he went back to talking so you could understand what he was saying.

Brother Roy Dodd explained that the "tongue" was a gift only a blessed few received. I asked the Lord to forgive me, but I was deeply hopeful at that moment I would never be so blessed. I was afraid I might get in the spirit and never get out.

A couple of years later, there was one more excitement at Brother Roy Dodd's revival. In the middle of one of Brother Roy

Dodd's sermons, a man stood up in the back and shouted, "Brother Roy Dodd! Have you ever taken up the serpent?"

Brother Roy Dodd said he hadn't.

"Would you take up the serpent to prove your faith?" asked the man.

"Never been asked to," answered Brother Roy Dodd.

"Well, I'm asking you now!" bellowed the man, who rushed toward the pulpit with a wrinkled brown sack in his hand. He dumped the contents of the sack at Brother Roy Dodd's feet and the crowd gasped. Out of the sack came a cottonmouth moccasin of some size. The snake did not appear to be overjoyed with the fact it was currently involved in a religious experience.

I knew all about taking up the serpent. It had been in the papers. There was a sect that believed a certain passage of the Bible beseeched a man to hold a snake to prove his faith. The papers had a story about a man who had been bitten recently by a timber rattler during services over at a church in Talbot County. The faithless scoundrel nearly died.

Brother Roy Dodd wasted little time in dealing with the snake. He picked up a metal folding chair in front of the piano, the one his wife Dora had vacated immediately upon seeing the snake, and beat hell and guts out of it.

When the snake was no longer moving, Brother Roy Dodd picked it up and held it before the stunned crowd.

"Shame I didn't have a chance to save this belly-crawling sinner before the Lord called him home," said Brother Roy Dodd.

The crowds began falling off for Brother Roy Dodd as the years passed. He added a healing segment to his performance to try to pick things up.

Miss Inez Pickett, a stout woman in her late fifties, came to see Brother Roy Dodd one night, complaining of what women used to call "the old mess," some sort of kidney disorder that was usually only whispered about.

Brother Roy Dodd, dressed in a sequin jacket he'd held on to since his singing days, asked Miss Inez where it hurt.

"My back," said Miss Inez.

Brother Roy Dodd put his hands firmly on Miss Inez's back and shook her kidneys with great force as he prayed.

"Did you feel that, Sister Inez?" asked Brother Roy Dodd.

"Lord Godamighty, I think I did!" shouted Miss Inez.

"You're healed!" said Brother Roy Dodd.

Miss Inez, plagued by her infirmity for many years, bounded about the platform in the manner of a much younger woman and made a number of joyful noises. I was afraid she was going to break into tongue.

Instead, she fell off the platform in her excitement, and you could hear the bone snap in her leg.

"Somebody call an ambulance!" the first one to her said.

"No need to do that," said somebody else. "Just get Brother Roy Dodd to give her another healing."

"Don't do no broke bones," said Brother Roy Dodd. "Just vital organs."

I was sixteen the summer Brother Roy Dodd didn't come back anymore. We heard all sorts of things. Nora and Cora left him for good, they said. Dora, his wife, got sick and couldn't play piano anymore. There was even something about a sheriff down in Mississippi someplace finding some white liquor on Brother Roy Dodd's bus.

That was a long summer, that summer Brother Roy Dodd didn't come back. We just sort of sat around and waited for fall and the fair and the geek who bit the heads off live chickens.

* * *

Talking to my preacher was my last order of business before getting on with the matter of the surgery on my heart.

I had heard all the statistics. Emory Hospital's most recent figures concerning heart surgery were quite favorable. The mortality rate was under three percent, and that included those who went to the table in desperate conditions.

One of my doctors had also assured me of the relative safety of the operation. He said there is always the unknown factor, but in many ways, when a person goes through surgery, he or she is safer than at any other time of his or her life because every part of the body is being closely monitored.

I was only thirty-five. They had called me an "excellent surgical risk." Still there was no absolute guarantee I might not wind up Emory's Upset Special of the Week, so I did, in fact, have to deal with the possibility my end might be near.

I had my will drawn up before I went to the hospital. Wills always begin by making reference to the fact the person about to dole out his life's belongings in the event of his demise is sound of mind. A person with complete control of his faculties wouldn't do such a thing in the first place.

Making out a will is depressing. I'll be honest. When it comes down to it, you really do want to take it with you.

Take my red coat. The Christmas before, I received the gift of a red ultra-suede sports jacket. I don't know exactly where I was supposed to wear a red, ultra-suede sports jacket since I don't attend Shriners' conventions, but it was a rather spiffy jacket, nonetheless.

I had shown it to a friend earlier, who was quite impressed.

"Wish I had a coat like that," he said.

"Where would you wear it?" I asked, just for the record.

"Next Shriners' convention," he said.

My friend came to visit soon after he found out about my impending heart surgery.

"Don't worry about a thing," he said. "People go through these operations all the time. It's a piece of cake."

You would be surprised how many people told me how easy heart surgery was going to be before I went to have heart surgery. Most of them, incidentally, had never been through medical procedures any more serious than offering a urine specimen.

"Still got that red coat?" my friend asked. I began to catch his drift.

"Still got it," I said. "Why do you ask?"

"Well, you never know about these things. I was just thinking that if you didn't make it through—not that there's one in a million chances you won't—maybe I could have your red coat."

One thing I made certain of in my will. Nobody got my red coat in case I bought the farm during my heart surgery. I left strict instructions I be buried in it.

My minister and I were alone in the hospital room. I was stretched out on the bed. He pulled his chair alongside me. A good preacher has a way about him, a way that calms.

First, we had a long discussion about hell. Hell has always confused me. Who goes to hell? Hitler, of course. Bonnie and Clyde must be there. There was a man in my hometown who shot at dogs for sport. My cousin had a fluffy little dog named Snowball and the man shot my cousin's dog dead.

"I hope he burns in hell for shooting my dog," said my cousin.

"On the same spit with Hitler and Bonnie and Clyde," I added.

As a kid, I always wondered exactly where hell was. Heaven is up; hell is down. But down where?

I used to wonder if you could dig your way to hell. I asked my minister about it.

"You probably can," he agreed. "But there are quicker ways to get there."

That brought up the current state of my status with the Lord.

"I haven't exactly been faithful," I said.

"None of us have," said my minister.

"I don't think you understand," I went on. "At last count, I had violated eight of the original Ten Commandments and had strongly considered the other two."

My preacher talked about forgiveness. He talked about it for a long time. Brother Roy Dodd couldn't have explained it any better. I listened closely. When he finished, I said, "Then you think if I don't make it through the operation tomorrow, there's still time for me to be forgiven for all the things I've done wrong?"

He looked at his watch.

"There's still time," he said, "but I'd get on it right away."

We prayed together before he left. He asked God to watch over me during the operation. I wanted him to ask God to have a sense of humor when he looked over my past life, but he didn't ask that.

I got out of my bed as the preacher began to leave. Family and friends were outside waiting.

First, I shook his hand. Then, I reached my arms around him, and he reached his arms around me.

Compared to the comfort and assurance of resting in the loving arms of a man of God for a few moments, Valium is child's play.

11

One of the editors of The Christian Century *told me that she has more difficulty obtaining religious humor for her magazine than any other type of writing. There is always a fine line, especially when one is writing about serious matters, between comedy and tragedy. There are always those who consider laughter about any serious issue or churchly concern to be impious.*

While I don't consider myself to be a worthy companion of the great humorists in this volume, I offer some little essays of my own as examples of a contemporary attempt at religious humor.

"THE EVANGELIZATION OF A FAMILY NAMED FULP"*

A Parable, with Apologies to E. B. White and the Church Growth Movement

William H. Willimon

In a sparsely populated corner of southern Iowa there lived a farm family by the name of Fulp. There were six Fulps. They farmed a hundred-acre plot of corn wedged between broad expanses of wheatfields, with an occasional house. The Fulps subsisted on what they grew in their garden, plus canned salmon, three turkeys a year, shredded wheat and one carton of soft drinks per week.

The Fulps were contented folk who minded their own

business and gave rides to hitchhikers (if they passed any) when they drove their pickup truck into town (seven miles away) for groceries each Saturday afternoon. They usually voted a straight Republican ticket. On the Fourth of July they set off a few firecrackers. In winter they mostly sat by the fire and watched reruns of "Gilligan's Island" and had popcorn and hot chocolate. On Saturday evenings, after all the little Fulps were in bed, Mr. and Mrs. Fulp each had a glass of Mogen David before retiring. On Sundays they slept late, occasionally arising in time to watch Oral Roberts.

No Fulp had ever been a member of anything—except for Mr. Fulp's brief stint in the American Legion after the war. The Fulps were not opposed to clubs or organized activities; the fact of the matter was that they had never been moved to seek membership. When a Fulp felt the need of companionship or intellectual stimulation, he or she simply sat down with another Fulp or else forgot about it.

I

One October, the Methodist, Baptist and Presbyterian churches in town got worked up over evangelism and launched a big community crusade to attract the unchurched. The Lutherans were worked up too, but since they were between pastors, they did not participate. The churches rented a billboard on the road into town and posted a message for the unchurched with a phone number for them to call if they were interested. The churches also took out a full-page ad in the weekly newspaper listing the hours when they had worship services. Prayer and study groups met each week in members' homes in town, to study why the unchurched were that way and to pray that they would change. They studied a book by a religion professor at Wilson College, available for $3.50 from Artos Publishers, Inc.

The Methodists and Baptists met each night for a week, sang some songs, prayed, took up a collection, and heard an evangelist from Texas who told them that their churches would "dry up and die" and be "as bad off as the Episcopalians" if they did not get some new members and if there was not a "rebirth of commitment to Christ." The Methodists hired an expert from Nashville who came in for a day and told them about the Church Growth Movement and said that what they needed to do was to reach out and love and go to where the people were. The Methodists decided to start a bridge club in their fellowship hall for the town's senior citizens.

As for the Baptists, they hired a man from Nashville who came in for a day and told them that what they needed was to do a community religious survey to determine where the un-churched were, to ask them why they were unchurched, and to get them churched. The Baptists did the survey, knocking on every door within a ten-mile radius. The survey revealed that the pickings were slim, so far as the unchurched were concerned. One lapsed Roman Catholic, an angry Baptist who was still mad about having lost out in the row over the church parking lot, and a woman who said that she went out of town to visit her aunt every weekend—these were the sole prospects to be found.

Except for a family outside of town by the name of Fulp.

When two women from the Baptist church, accompanied by a woman from the Presbyterian chuch, called on the Fulps, they were welcomed warmly by Mrs. Fulp, who offered them coffee, and by the little Fulps, who, in responding to the women's questions, informed them that they were five, eight, ten and 14 respectively and that Mr. Fulp was fixing the gears on the tractor. After a while, Mr. Fulp came in and the women talked to him too.

The women, upon discovering that the Fulps were utterly unchurched, encouraged them to decide on one of the town's churches and to start attending. They also urged the little Fulps to come to Sunday school where they would be with lots of other nice boys and girls. The Presbyterian admitted that her church had too few children to have a Sunday school but added that they did have a nice young minister fresh out of seminary. One of the leaders from the Baptist church told Mrs. Fulp that the Baptists taught only the Bible in their Sunday school and that their church youth group went on a choir tour to New Orleans every spring.

The Fulps listened politely, asked no questions, thanked the women for coming, and told them to come back any time they wished. Mr. Fulp excused himself and went back out to work on the tractor.

II

Rushing back into town, the women alerted their pastors to the plight of the Fulps. One said she detected that the Fulps seemed to be searching for something. Another visitor noted that Mrs. Fulp had a pleasant voice and could probably sing in a church choir. The pastors speculated that Mr. Fulp was probably your irresponsible type of father but that he could possibly be reached if he were visited by a couple of businessmen from town.

The response of the churches and their members was immediate and gratifying. A prayer group covenanted to pray for the Fulps each day, at noon and at 4:30. The owner of the Ford dealership in town volunteered to call on Mr. Fulp, while a delegation of women called on Mrs. Fulp on six separate occasions, taking her a chocolate pie and a cassette recording of an inspirational address by Dale Evans. Members of the youth group at the Baptist church decided to adopt the Fulps as their fall project and to have a party for the two older Fulp children. The Methodists focused on the two younger Fulps, mailing them a "We Missed You" postcard each Sunday after Sunday school. Local merchants were asked to watch for the Fulps when they came into town on Saturday afternoons and to try to get a commitment from them to attend church the next day.

All of the ministers called upon the Fulps every week, each one leaving a stack of membership materials from his church and a copy of the *Upper Room*. The Methodist minister spent an afternoon explaining, in some detail, the Methodist Social Principles and clarifying why the church's General Board of

Discipleship had gone on record recently in favor of binding arbitration in labor disputes.

The Fulps themselves were a bit overwhelmed by all the attention. The little Fulps started attending church, which meant that they were hardly ever home anymore. Mrs. Fulp now spent most of her day on the telephone talking to the women from the various churches or else listening to her latest cassette of *The Total Woman*. Mr. Fulp stopped making the weekly pilgrimage into town on Saturday with his family since he felt harassed in every store where they shopped. He also started avoiding Mrs. Fulp after she returned from town one Saturday with a pair of hot-pink baby-doll pajamas. Eventually, Mr. and Mrs. Fulp stopped speaking to each other altogether after a three-hour argument one night over prevenient grace. The 14-year-old Fulp, who had learned to smoke on a recent youth retreat, was becoming insufferably rebellious.

III

Finally, the pressure got to Mr. Fulp. One night, after their new practice of family devotionals, he climbed into his pickup truck and headed for Des Moines, never to be heard from again. It is assumed that he probably perished there as a wino, following several months of dissipation. The younger Fulps became regular Sunday school attenders, two at the Baptist church and one at the Methodist church. The eldest Fulp offspring ran away with a 17-year-old majorette while they were in New Orleans together on the spring choir tour. From New Orleans they made their way to California, where it is rumored that they now live together out of wedlock.

Mrs. Fulp sold the farm and moved into town where she was led to join the Presbyterian church, an action on her part which led nearly half of the women in town to vow never to speak to her again and which led the Methodist minister to phone the Presbyterian minister and tell him what he thought of his proselyting. The Baptist minister said that he had detected, early in his acquaintance with Mrs. Fulp, that she was emotionally unstable and he hoped that the Presbyterians could give her whatever it was that she was looking for.

Mrs. Fulp now does workshops in Parent Effectiveness Training and can be booked through the Presbyterian synod office at 203 Maguire Street, Iowa City, Iowa 52240.

12

"THE MICROCHIP CHURCH"*

William H. Willimon

There was this boy in my class in high school. He was the most out-of-it person I knew. He wore shoes with laces, white shirts and white socks, and used Vitalis. He was always talking about how interesting some algebra problem was on last night's homework.

You can imagine my surprise on meeting this fellow at a high-school reunion and learning that he now lives in California overlooking the beach—one of those exclusive places where everyone is into consciousness-raising and owns a Doberman. He came to the reunion with a beard and blue jeans and driving a Rolls. It turns out that this guy has invented a computer game. He thought it up one night while watching "Family Feud." He programmed the game that night after the show, set up his own company the next morning, and had already sold over $2 million worth of stock before dinner that evening. By the next day the stock had divided twice; needless to say, he is now very, very well off. I haven't actually seen the game, but it is something about a family of gnomes who are trying to find the Holy Grail through a maze of monsters.

He is now working on a game he wouldn't say much about, in which the gnomes set up a theme amusement park after they find the Grail. The computer takes them through the adventures of setting up their own corporation. Atari is said to be positively frantic over the prospect.

So I went home from the high-school reunion depressed as the devil. "That could have been me," I thought.

Why him? Sure, I was never too good in algebra, but I've always had a storehouse of good ideas. Look at me, 38, living in a Methodist parsonage and driving a Dart. Look who's Mr. Out-of-It now. There is the fabulous, brave new world of computers and here is the church. There is Columbus launching out into unexplored territory and here I am, staying home, perfecting the Gregorian chant.

But that was yesterday. You've heard of the electronic church. Well, I now serve the first microchip church. While other pastors are sipping coffee at Ministerial Association meetings and visiting nursing homes, I have been quietly putting together a computerized ministry conglomerate. Friends ask, "How do you do it?" It's a simple blend of economic savvy and good old American ingenuity.

It is somewhat odd that I should be presiding over a multimillion-dollar church. In seminary, nobody thought that I showed much promise for ministry. One of my professors told me after I took his liturgics exam that I ought to consider using my talents in real estate rather than in administering the Eucharist.

My entry into the new age of computers began when I contemplated leading the upcoming fall Bible study group, a job I've always detested. As always, it was going to be on Paul. I thought of all those long hours in the church parlor getting more and more depressed at the idea. Then it occured to me: Why not devise a game to do it for me—a "Pac-Man" for Paul?

I took a crash course in programming at our local Radio Shack. In two weeks, I had what is, as far as I know, the first computerized Bible action game. Using a little stick and a television screen, the computer takes a tiny Paul on his journey through Asia Minor. Jail, beatings, thorns in the flesh, Judaizers, the circumcision party—they're all there. The player has to figure out how Paul is going to make it to his heavenly reward in Rome.

The United Methodist Bible study group loved it. They would never go back to the old way of Bible study. The church parlor, which used to be adorned with large wing chairs, two sofas and a Sallman's *Head of Christ,* is now this country's first Christian video arcade. I have since added a number of neat games such as "Samson and the Philistines" and "Ten Difficult Sayings of Jesus Made Easy." Needless to say, the kids love it. How many churches do you know that have to run the teen-agers out of the church in the evening in order to lock up?

We are now negotiating with a number of denominational publishing houses to market our line of Bible-based video games, although Sears may be our best prospect. I predict that in four or five years the familiar Sunday-school quarterly will be as antiquated as a Temperance Society pledge card is today and my church, thanks to royalties and residuals from our software, will make the income of the Crystal Cathedral look like that of the little church in the wildwood.

Things went so well with our first foray into the world of computers that we decided to computerize everything in the church. We bought a new IBM system with terminals in all the church offices. As a means of pastoral care, the computer is virtually limitless. Everybody in my church is now on our computer, with their complete personal information and record of giving. At the punch of a button we can send everyone a birthday card, anniversary card, recognition of any personal event in their lives, or a reminder of how far behind they are on their pledge. Every day our computer pulls people's names and makes a personal call to them (using a recording of my voice) which goes something like this: "Hello, [name inserted]. This is your pastor. Just wanted you to know that I was thinking about you in my prayer time this morning. Isn't this the day you married [or divorced, were robbed, graduated, got certified, were promoted, or fired, or 200 other categories of human experience] last year? Why, certainly I remembered. How could I forget? Good-bye, (X)."

How many traditionalist pastors do you know who can do this?

Our computer is now our number-one evangelism aid. We have an on-line connection with the local police station, family court, credit bureau and electric company. We receive a printout each day of everyone who moves into town, everyone who is arrested, all filings for divorce and child custody, and upcoming cases in civil court. Talk about matching the gospel to human need! Imagine the impression we make on a family who has just had the lights turned off for nonpayment of their electric bill when a church team shows up offering to have prayer with them. A year ago, we couldn't have done that.

We also utilize our electronic genius for more activist concerns. Within minutes I can send personal letters to every congressperson in our state's delegation, each letter signed by a member of our congregation, protesting some pending legislation. Can you imagine the impact on a politician of receiving a thousand letters in a day expressing righteous indignation over his vote yesterday?

When the bishop tried to move me last year because of the complaints of a group of malcontents in the congregation—conservative Neanderthals who don't know a cathode-ray tube from a concordance—guess who got a thousand personal letters expressing shock and dismay? We are also able to send personalized sympathy cards and get-well cards to any district superintendent in our conference. Some people sit around and wait for the Holy Spirit to work; I prefer to peck out new programs that make a few things happen when they ought to.

While other pastors are pounding the pavement, knocking on doors, beating out sermons, I have just sent letters to every charismatic female over the age of 35 with a college degree who owns her own home and has an income of over $30,000 a year, to tell each one personally about our special upcoming Labor Day service. I am writing this article on my word processor, which automatically filters out bad spelling, incorrect grammar and homiletical clichés—at the touch of a button.

Think of what Martin Luther could have done with this technology!

13

"THE AMERICAN WAY"*

William H. Willimon

I'm always surprised by the biblical belief that the persistent, unconquerable sin is hubris, pride. I am surprised not because I am free of pride but because the Lord has so many effective means to cure me of it. Whenever I get really good at clerical hubris, along comes God, and I see my nakedness, my Tower of Babel crashes, and I am driven back to grace.

The other day I received a telephone call from a man in a nearby town. "I read an article of yours and really appreciated it. I would like to discuss a related matter with you. In view of your writing, I think you'll be interested in an idea of mine."

Naturally, I was flattered. It's always good to hear that one's thoughts have moved someone else to thought or action. I looked forward to our Monday afternoon meeting where we could explore further our mutual concerns. I told my secretary to hold my calls once the admirer arrived.

At 1:30 P.M. a young man entered my office, introduced himself, took charge, loosened his polyester tie, took a chair, moved it close to mine and began to speak. "I'll need just 15 minutes of your time. Please allow me to explain my ideas fully, and then we can talk."

---

*Copyright 1982 Christian Century Foundation. Reprinted by permission from the October 13, 1982, issue of *The Christian Century*.

I listened intently, watching as he drew circles and lines on a paper. "I can see from your writing that you want to help people," he said. I had never received that particular compliment on my writing, but I thought about it as he continued, and I agreed that I did indeed wish to help people.

"I can see from your writing you are a man of action." I continued to listen.

"All you do is to simply get six other people who want to increase their independence—and help others. You can do this in your free time, in your own home," he said.

"Wait a minute," I said. "This sounds like some sort of pyramid sales scheme, like Amway or something."

"This is not a 'scheme,' but this is Amway," he replied. "Will you please allow me to finish my talk?"

"You mean you have come here to get me to sell Amway? Soap? Detergent? Wax?"

"No, I've come here to invite you to be an Amway distributor."

"But I'm a United Methodist pastor. I've got my hands full with this crowd here without selling toilet bowl cleaner too."

"I have preachers who work for Amway," he said, "even doctors, no less. A Baptist preacher in Atlanta does our tapes."

"That's fine for them, but not for me."

"Look," he said, "you must have gotten the wrong impression about Amway. Don't you believe in the American free-enterprise system? This is all Amway is about. We're pushing the American Way. Get it? Amway."

"I *did* believe in the American free-enterprise system—that is, before this discussion began."

"If you don't want to help other people achieve financial independence, don't you want independence for yourself? As far as I can tell, you're in a risky position, having your financial future tied to the whims of a church committee."

"Now cut that out! First you come in here appealing to my altruism. Now you're appealing to my capitalistic greed. This really *is* sounding like the American Way! I told you I'm not interested." My color was changing from pastoral pink to Marxist red.

"Dr. Willimon, it's just like Jesus said," he continued.

"Like Jesus said about what?" I asked.

" 'Where there is no vision, the people perish.' All I'm trying to do is to give you a vision of the financial independence you can have through the wonderful world of Amway."

"You dummy, Jesus didn't say that. That's from the Old Testament. What about 'Go, sell all you have and give to the poor'?" I asked triumphantly.

He was undeterred. "I expect Amway saves more people every day than your average church—certainly more than this church."

"Out! Out!" I was screaming now.

"Sorry, Dr. Willimon. You write good, but you'll never be another Norman Vincent Peale with a negative attitude like yours."

"Out! Out!"

He was pulling materials from his briefcase now. "Here's a good article on Amway from *Reader's Digest*. That ought to impress you."

"Out! Out!"

He finally gathered his notebooks and sales charts, moved reluctantly through the door and down the hall toward the parking lot, smiling condescendingly all the while.

My secretary sat in the outer office typing, fighting back a smirk. "We seem to be a little disturbed, don't we?" she observed.

"If anybody else calls, I'm out," I growled.

When and if I regain enough ego strength to preach or write, I shall do so as a committed Marxist. I must admit, however, that it gives me some comfort to know that if I fail at preaching the gospel, or if my bishop ever gives up on me, there is a place for me within the great American Way. I can quit preaching the way of Christ crucified and sell pine-scented cleaner instead.

14

"OLYMPICS FOR CLERICS"*

William H. Willimon

Picture yourself on a Sunday morning in the middle of the church service. With a considerable flourish, you have just announced that you are going to baptize a baby. The child's proud parents and godparents bring the infant forward while the congregation smiles. Two hundred pairs of eyes are on you as you put aside your worship book, lift the lid off the font and, to your horror, find that it is empty, bone dry, as desiccated as the Sahara.

Keeping your pleasant, unruffled, official clerical smile, you turn and say in a clear, resonant voice, "And now Jane Jones, our chairperson of the worship committee, will obtain the water."

Somewhat hesitantly, Jones moves from her seat. Reassured by your smile and confidence, she leaves the sanctuary, goes to the women's room, fills a pitcher with water, returns and hands it to you. As you take it, you ask the congregation to bow while you say a short prayer about the "freshness of water."

The parents, godparents and congregation participate in the succeeding ritual with no apparent awareness that anything was amiss. In fact, a number of people in the congregation whisper their approval of this addition to the Service of Christian Baptism.

Then at the rear of the church five people stand up, each holding a large white card reading, respectively, 4, 5, 4, 4, 5—near perfect score for a nearly faultless performance in a tough situation. You have taken the lead in the emergency liturgical adaptation competition.

This stirring spectacle was recently enacted in Pasadena, California, at the First Clergy Olympiad, sponsored by the Greater Pasadena Council of Churches. It is the brainchild of the Rev. Dr. John Winterbottom, who, inspired by the 1984 Olympics to be held in Los Angeles, organized this gathering of the nation's best pastors.

"It all started with a dream of mine," said Winterbottom. "I was home one night eating tacos with my wife and kids when the idea came to me. I said to myself, 'How come we preachers never get a chance to show just how good we are at what we do?' The average person has no idea of the demands of the parish ministry, the kinds of pressures we are under, the heroic acts that we do every day, without congregational recognition."

This put Winterbottom on the way to founding the Clergy Olympiad. "We needed some way to recognize and improve the work that pastors do. This event is our way of saying, 'Hey, world, these guys and gals know what they're doing and they are damn good at it.' "

Clergy from nearly 30 states were present for the beginning of the four-day competition. Most of the participants were Protestant, with evangelicals having the largest representation and taking the most gold medals. Though the event failed to win the official approval of the Vatican, a number of Roman Catholic observers attended this year's games.

You really get to see the quality of the work that's being done in the field," said on layperson from Ventura. "There are some real professionals here. I've noted that the evangelicals seem to have it over the liberals. I think that they are a little more competitive, a little less prone to 'turn the other cheek' as far as professional competition goes."

While space limitations prohibit my describing all aspects of the Olympiad in detail, here are a few of the highlights. Jane

Smith, though in her late 30s, easily won the calling-card dash. In this event, participants must run from their parked automobiles up a 70-foot walkway, ring a doorbell, leave their calling cards tucked firmly in the door and get back into their cars before the inhabitants of the home have time to answer the bell.

Smith, a Presbyterian from Kansas, said that she entered the ministry comparatively late in life. This makes her performance in this event particularly noteworthy. "I serve a rather large parish," she explained. "And, being a woman, I have to work just a little bit harder than most men in order to prove myself." She had no trouble besting her male competitors in this event.

As was to be expected, Episcopalians dominated the field in liturgical contests such as the serving of the Eucharist. United Methodists made a surprisingly good showing in the confirmation marathon, a grueling, nonstop endurance test in which a pastor has to give three lectures on history, doctrine and polity to a group of fifth- and sixth-graders. Since confirmation is a comparatively recent phenomenon among United Methodists, their superb performance clearly caught the Lutherans and Episcopalians off guard. "Well, they have less history, doctrine and polity than we do," commented a disgruntled member of the Lutheran team.

The potluck relay required pastors to hurry down the serving line of a typical potluck dinner heaping their plates with at least ten items while avoiding Swedish meatballs and tuna surprise.

But the event that everyone in the crowd eagerly awaited was the clergy decathlon. This contest lumped together a score of torturous, demanding clerical skills in a two-hour test of endurance. Perhaps because of their belief in economic competition and in the body as a temple, the evangelicals took the field here. The Methodists looked good in the first event—filling out year-end reports, an area in which Baptists seem to have little experience. Baptists, Methodists and Presbyterians fell behind in the liturgical-vesting competition. But it was the UCCs who were in the cellar on this one. The two competitors from Wisconsin dropped hopelessly behind when they were unable to tell the front from the back of a damask chasuble.

By the time the decathlon moved into such tests as the preaching-volume throw and the tedious-member vault, Baptists commanded an easy lead. Although they stumbled in the doctrinal-disagreement hurdles, these more conservative pastors had smooth sailing through the rest of the decathlon.

All in all, it was a wonderful occasion. Participants went away with a better appreciation of each other's cultural and theological differences and similarities. Spectators were unanimous in their praise for the pastors.

"I just never knew that being a pastor was so tough," said an observing seminarian from Melodyland. "I'm going back to my studies with a new sense of dedication. Who knows, maybe someday I'll be the first Pentecostal to take a gold medal in the doctrinal-disagreement hurdles."

Such comments made all the struggle, hard work and derision worthwhile to Dr. Winterbottom. Said Winterbottom: "Right now, out in Iowa or someplace like that, some unknown, unheralded pastor is going about his or her duties, dreaming of the time that he or she will be good enough to compete with the greats at the Clergy Olympiad II. Maybe that dream will keep that pastor going."

The next Olympiad is scheduled to be held in either Nashville, Tennessee, or Tulsa, Oklahoma.

15

"METHODIST PREACHERS"*

William H. Willimon

In the winter of 1740, when our nation was still a wild frontier and Horry County was even more uncivilized than it is today, the Reverend Dr. George Whitefield preached his way through South Carolina up the coast from Charleston. Whitefield was already the rage of England. An English actor of the day, David Garrick, claimed that Whitefield could bring a congregation to its knees in tears just by the mere pronunciation of "Mesopotamia" from his lips. Whitefield was a leader in the rapidly spreading Methodist movement there and was now in the colonies helping launch what would come to be called the "First Great Awakening."

In Charleston, Whitefield received a rather icy reception from the Episcopalians who distrusted what they called his "dangerous enthusiasm." Old Alexander Garden called him a "rascal." But, you know how Charleston Episcopalians are. Even the slightest expression of liveliness may be judged "dangerous" by them. At any rate, Whitefield was virtually run out of Charleston, a city which managed then as now to be unimpressed with just about everyone and everything that does not originate in Charleston. And so he made his way up the

*From *Family, Friends, and Other Funny People: Memories of Growing Up Southern* by William H. Willimon and Harriet Willimon Cabell. Copyright, 1980, by William H. Willimon, Sandlapper Books, Orangeburg, S.C. Used by permission.

coast, arriving in the vicinity of what is now Little River, South Carolina, on New Year's Eve of 1740.

As I noted earlier, the stretch from Myrtle Beach to Little River today often impresses outsiders as being uncivilized and pagan. It impressed Whitefield exactly that same way—and, mind you, this was in 1740, even before the miniature golf courses and discothèques. It was a wild, unreligious, rowdy sort of place even then. Whitefield records in his diary how hard his journey was from Georgetown to Little River—and he did not even have to contend with travel trailers, mobile homes, and New Jersey tourists on Highway 17. At last, on New Year's Eve, he came upon a crossroads tavern near Little River where he decided to spend the night.

It was afternoon, but already the drinking, dancing, and carousing had begun. The locals were bringing in 1741 with the kind of raucous abandon which was eventually to become legendary among later visitors to the Grand Strand. Whitefield was deeply disturbed. No sooner had he put down his bags than he went to work exhorting the astonished revelers with every homiletical device at his disposal.

Evidently the traveling preacher was effective, for his listeners were moved from their initial shock and anger to penitence and contrition. Benjamin Franklin records having heard Whitefield preach in Philadelphia and deemed him to be one of the finest preachers of the century. The natives at the tavern that night must have agreed, for they were visibly moved. Whitefield noted in his diary that most of them were converted that night and a number came forward for baptism. He baptized them, instructed them in the virtues of an upright and sober life, and then, blessing them in their new life and change of heart, he retired for the night, joyful in his success at converting these Carolina pagans.

Whitefield ends his account of his evening at Little River thus: "Sometime after midnight I was awakened by the sound of loud music and raucous merrymaking downstairs. The dancing and drinking had resumed."

That night, the Reverend Dr. George Whitefield found what

later generations of Methodist preachers who followed him to the wilds of South Carolina were to discover: the conversion and sanctification of Sandlappers is no easy task. Subsequent Methodist preachers may feel that they have had as short-lived an influence on the mores and morals of Carolinians as Whitefield's New Year's Eve sermon.

However, in this essay I will argue that Methodist preachers have been a distinct breed within our state and that their influence has been great even though it has been often overlooked. To the uninformed, Methodist preachers are often dismissed as fried-chicken-eating, loud-preaching, golf-playing parsons. I will not deny that most Methodist preachers do have an acknowledged propensity for fried chicken, nor would I urge the merely casual golfer to make any sort of wager with a Methodist preacher on a turn around the links. But more must be said about the personalities of these "traveling preachers." It should be admitted at the outset that I make no claims of objectivity here. I am a Methodist preacher myself and my father-in-law and step-grandmother-in-law are both Methodist preachers in South Carolina. Of course, I know there are those who will agree with my Aunt Agnes who said, when told that I planned to enter seminary to prepare myself for ministry in the Methodist church, "I have never met a Methodist preacher who had good sense."

Just for the record, it should be noted that my Aunt Agnes was a Presbyterian, so one can hardly expect objectivity on her part either. It should also be said that, although I could serve gladly in many denominations, I would probably not choose to serve among the Presbyterians. You will probably think that this is not a very objective attitude on my part but then, the only Presbyterian I knew when I was growing up was my Aunt Agnes and, if you had known her, you would not be very objective about Presbyterians either.

Before attempting to understand South Carolina Methodist preachers, one must have some appreciation for Methodist history in our state and at least a rudimentary understanding of Methodist polity.

Methodists are organized (using the term *organized* rather

loosely) into Annual Conferences. All Methodists in South Carolina are part of the South Carolina Annual Conference. It was not always so. Until the early part of this century, South Carolina Methodists were grouped into two conferences, the Upper South Carolina Annual Conference and the Lower South Carolina Annual Conference. Eventually they were merged into one conference. The merger was rather controversial and there was heated debate—as there always is whenever Methodists do anything. Methodist preachers in the upper half of the state were concerned about the use of tobacco among their fellow clergy in the lower half of the state. Methodist preachers in the lower half of the state were concerned about the poor theology of their fellow clergy in the upper half of the state. Methodist preachers in Charleston managed to be concerned about neither. For their part, they had taken it upon themselves to be concerned about the eternal destiny of Charleston Episcopalians—an issue which is never in doubt among Charleston Episcopalians but which has always troubled Charleston Methodists.

Methodist preachers are under the care (using the term *care* rather loosely) of someone called a "bishop." Bishops are Methodist preachers who are elected by their fellow Methodist preachers after an extensive election campaign for the office in which the candidate tries very hard to appear not to be campaigning. It is a long-standing Methodist tradition that bishops must not appear to have sought their office and, once elected, the new bishop must make a public declaraton that "I didn't seek this office and I didn't want it but, once the Lord calls . . ." Of course, Methodist preachers take all of this with a grain of salt, the same way Baptist congregations have learned to be somewhat skeptical when one of their preachers moves on to a better church claiming, "I hate to leave this church and I would rather stay here, but the Lord calls . . ." Baptists note that the Lord rarely calls someone out of one church into another church unless that church has a higher salary. Methodists have likewise noted that there have been few preachers who, once they are elected bishop, turn the job down.

Methodists are highly organized. They are known for doing things very "methodically"—hence the name, "Methodist." Of course, if you have ever attended an annual meeting of the South Carolina Annual Conference, you may challenge this claim of Methodist organization. Annual Conference meetings occur once a year, usually in Spartanburg or Columbia. All the Methodist preachers gather and pray, sing, listen to reports, argue, and do a great deal of politicking related to their pastoral appointments for the coming year. The preachers have a great time during all this but sometimes the lay delegates become rather disillusioned by all the hullabaloo and bickering that takes place during the business sessions. As one commentator observed, "Methodist preachers are like manure. Spread them around the state and they do a lot of good. Pile them together in one place and they get to stinking."

The end of Annual Conference comes when the bishop reads out each minister's appointment for the coming year. The entire conference sits in hushed anticipation as each pastor is told where he or she will be serving. The pastors ready themselves to go willingly to any church the bishop has decided they should serve. At least, that is supposed to be the way it happens. I remember the year when one preacher's response at the reading of his appointment was to shout to his wife seated next to him, "Oh, Mama, they've ruined us!" and to fall over in a dead faint.

In all fairness to the churches where the preachers are being sent, it should be noted that some of these congregations are none too happy over who the bishop sends them either. I heard about some wretched little town somewhere that had a great reputation for meanness. In the early part of the last century there had been a number of killings in the town, beatings were an everyday occurence, and lawlessness was the order of the day. Religion was the last thing these frontier roughnecks had on their minds. Thus you can understand how frightened the young Methodist circuit rider was when he was sent by his bishop to try to form a church in this hostile place. The young minister entered the town's only pulpit with fear and trembling.

He looked out upon two dozen hostile, mean-looking faces. He was shaking so much that he could barely hold his Bible but he went ahead and managed to preach his sermon. When his sermon ended, there was utter silence. Then, one of the meanest of the mean-looking characters swaggered up to him and said, "Son, you don't have to worry, we ain't going to hurt you. But we aim to shoot that no good rascal what sent you here to us." Being a bishop has it difficulties.

The story is told of the Methodist preacher who, having been told at conference that he was to move, returned to his church to preach his farewell sermon on his last Sunday there. At the end of his sermon, he took his place at the door of the church and bid farewell to his parishioners. He noticed that one poor woman was weeping uncontrollably, obviously in a state of grief at his leaving.

"Don't cry, sister," he said in an attempt to comfort the woman. "You know that even though I am leaving, the bishop is going to send you a fine preacher."

"Yes," the woman said through her tears. "That's what they've been telling this church for twenty years and it ain't happened yet."

Of course, attending to the spiritual affairs of people is no easy matter. But most Methodist preachers will go to great lengths to raise the moral life of their parishioners. Consider the case of the Methodist preacher near Darlington who, having driven his old Ford to its grave while going about his pastoral duties, was generously offered the gift of a used car to replace his Ford. A parishioner offered to take the preacher over to Darlington to buy him one of the used cars at the auction. The preacher and his parishioner sat in the bidder's gallery and watched as the cars rolled by and were bidded on, waiting for one that looked suitably inexpensive and ecclesiastically conservative. The preacher excused himself, left his friend, made his way down to the professional auto buyers who were gathered on the first row of the gallery and started a conversation with the car dealers.

"You see that old Chevrolet getting ready to come down the

line?" the preacher asked the dealers. They nodded in response. "How much would you fellas think that car will bring?"

"Five hundred dollars," the dealers all agreed.

The preacher returned to his seat next to his friend in the gallery and they continued to talk of this and that.

"See that old Chevrolet getting ready to be auctioned?" the preacher asked his friend.

"Yes."

"How much do you think it will bring?"

"Not over $250, at the most," declared the parishioner.

"Oh, I bet it could bring $500," the preacher responded.

"Now, preacher, you don't know nothing about cars. That old heap will be lucky to bring $250."

"Well, you may be right," the preacher continued, "but I still say I bet it will bring about $500."

"Would you like to put a little money behind that bet?" challenged the parishioner (who was beginning to get a little heated over the matter).

"Sure, I'll bet you $50 that Chevrolet will bring more than you think."

They shook hands on the bet. The Chevrolet came up for auction and immediately was sold for just over $500. The layman was shocked.

"How did you get to know so much about car deals?" he asked his preacher in astonishment.

"Never you mind that," responded the preacher. "You just hand over that $50 and let this be a lesson to you never to gamble again. It's a sin, you know."

As I said, Methodist preachers will go to great lengths to upgrade the morals of those who are entrusted to their care.

At one time, Methodists were nicknamed "Shouting Methodists"—a name which they earned not only by virtue of their usually emotional worship services but also because of the vocal capacities of their preachers. I remember the day when many Methodist preachers would consider it an affront to their preaching skills to suggest that they speak from a public address system. I know a man in Camden (a Baptist) who claims that his preacher used to have him stand on the front porch of his church listening for the Methodist preacher to begin to wind down his sermon so the man could signal his own preacher to end his sermon so that the Baptists could beat the Methodists to the front of the line at the local cafeteria. I was incredulous of this claim since the two churches are several blocks apart. However, the man added that this was summertime when the windows of the Methodist church were open. In winter, when the windows were closed, one had to be at least within a block of the church before the Methodist preacher could be heard.

I must confess that many Methodist sermons tend to be heavy on volume and emotion and a bit light on content. I remember the Methodist revivalist who was unable, in spite of his flailing arms and shouting and sweating, to stir the hearts of an intransigent congregation. In the midst of his efforts, an old dog wandered into the little church and began to howl. The horrified ushers moved quickly to eject the hound.

"Leave 'im alone," the preacher commanded from the pulpit. "That's probably the first tear that's been shed in this place for fifty years. There's hope for him, but I don't know about the rest of you."

Many laypersons have the erroneous notion that preachers live rather sheltered lives. This is untrue; after all, they are forced to live all over South Carolina during the course of their ministry, and this day-to-day contact with people from Tigerville to Timmonsville does not make for a fragile disposition. As my father-in-law used to say when he heard people criticize the unruly behavior of ministers' children, "Of course preachers' kids tend to be wild and unruly; they have to play with the children in the congregation, don't they?"

The story is told of the 250-pound Aiken Methodist preacher who picked up two young hitchhikers as he returned home from a visit to the Columbia hospital one day. No sooner were they in the car than they pulled a gun on him and asked for his wallet. He had already told them that he was a Methodist preacher so this request showed how dumb the two young brigands were. As one would expect, the wallet contained nothing but the preacher's driver's license, his membership card for the Aiken Ministerial Association and an overdue bill from an Aiken supermarket. They then, getting rough and angry with the preacher, forced him to turn off on a deserted country road where they planned to dispose of the preacher and use his car for some escapade.

When they were at an appropriately deserted spot, they told him to stop the car and get out. He obliged them. They got out and told him to lean against a nearby tree. One of the hoodlums held the preacher's hands behind his back while the other cocked the pistol and held it close to the preacher's head.

"Prepare to meet your God," the young man said. To which the preacher responded, "No, my son, I don't think I hear the Lord calling me just yet." He then leaned forward, pulling one of his captors off balance with him as he grabbed the gun from his other would-be assailant. He bashed their heads together, shook them both up and down a couple of times for good measure, tossed into the rear seat of his automobile and drove them to the hospital emergency room in Aiken. It is said that the preacher later converted the two young men in one of his many hospital visits to them, though it is not known whether their conversions from a life of crime were due to fear or faith.

"You can't spend your life serving Methodist churches in South Carolina without knowing how to take care of yourself," was all that the preacher had to say about the incident.

John Wesley, the founder of the Methodist movement in England, used to urge his preachers to "be in constant reading and study." Thus the erudition of Methodist preachers is a long-standing tradition.

Bishop Edward Tullis of South Carolina tells the story of a Kentucky Methodist preacher who went out deer hunting in the Kentucky woods. After two or three days of camping and hunting alone in the wilderness, late one afternoon he started back to where his car was parked. It was not long before he realized that he was walking in circles and that he was hopelessly lost in the woods. The highway and his car were nowhere to be seen. Darkness fell, and the preacher grew more concerned about his situation. He decided to fire his shotgun in hopes that someone might hear him and help him find his way back to the road. No sooner had he fired his gun a couple of times than a state game warden stepped out of the bush and arrested the forlorn preacher for hunting at night.

All of the minister's claims that he was lost proved to no avail. Besides as it turned out, he was only a few feet from the road and his car but had not known it. The game warden found it impossible to believe that the preacher had been lost and was determined to take the culprit to jail.

"But officer, I am the pastor of one of the most distinguished Methodist churches in this state," the preacher pleaded. The game warden focused his spotlight upon the man's unshaven face, looked over his dirty hunting outfit, and continued to be unconvinced that this bedraggled-looking fellow was a man of God.

"All right, if you are a Methodist preacher, then let me hear you repeat the words of the Lord's Prayer," said the game warden. The unnerved preacher began, "The Lord is my shepherd, I shall not want; he maketh me to lie down . . ."

"By God you *are* a Methodist preacher," confirmed the game warden.

16

The great American playwright and novelist Thornton Wilder frequently dealt with religious subjects. Never did Wilder create better humor, or more pointed criticism of American popular religion, than in his 1935 novel, Heaven's My Destination. *Wilder takes his sincere, devout, innocent, and maddening protagonist, George Brush, through an uproarious series of misadventures. In the first selection, poor Brush finds that conversion of the heathen is no easy matter. In the second selection, Brush precipitates a run on the local bank when, obeying Jesus' strictures against usury, he refuses to take the interest on his account which the bank tries to pay him. Life under the dictates of the Sermon on the Mount can be either tragic or comic—depending on one's point of view.*

ENCOUNTER WITH A PAGAN*

Thornton Wilder

One morning in the late summer of 1930 the proprietor and several guests at the Union Hotel at Crestcrego, Texas, were annoyed to discover Biblical texts freshly written across the blotter on the public writing-desk. Two days later the guests at McCarty's Inn, Usquepaw, in the same state, were similarly irritated, and the manager of the Gem Theater near by was surprised to discover that a poster at his door had been defaced and trampled upon. The same evening a young man passing the First Baptist Church, and seeing that the Annual Bible Question

*Abridged from pages 19-35 in *Heaven's My Destination* by Thornton Wilder. Copyright 1934, 1962 by Thornton Wilder. By permission of Harper & Row, Publishers.

Bee was in progress, paid his fifteen cents and, taking his place against the wall, won the first prize, his particular triumph being the genealogical tables of King David. The next night, several passengers on the Pullman car "Quarritch," leaving Fort Worth, were startled to discover a young man in pajamas kneeling and saying his prayers before his berth. His concentration was not shaken when he was struck sharply on the shoulder by flying copies of the *Western Magazine* and *Screen Features*. The next morning a young lady who had retired to the platform of the car to enjoy a meditative cigarette after breakfast, returned to her seat to discover a business card that had been inserted into the corner of the window pane. It read: *George Marvin Brush, Representing the Caulkins Educational Press, New York, Boston, and Chicago. Publishers of Caulkins' Arithmetics and Algebras, and other superior textbooks for school and college.* Across the top of the card the following words had been neatly added in pencil: *Women who smoke are unfit to be mothers.* The young lady reddened slightly, tore the card into flakes and pretended to go to sleep. After a few moments she sat up and, assuming an expression of weary scorn, looked about the car. None of the passengers seemed capable of such a message, least of all a tall, solidly built young man whose eyes, nevertheless, were gravely resting on her.

This young man, feeling that he had made his point, picked up his briefcase and went forward to the smoking-car. There almost every seat was filled. The day was already hot and the smokers, having discarded coat and collar, lay sprawled about in the blue haze. Several card games were in progress, and in one corner an excitable young man was singing an interminable ballad, alternately snapping his fingers and stamping his heel to mark the beat. An admiring group was gathered about him, supplying the refrain. Congeniality already reigned in the car and remarks were being shouted from one end of it to the other. Brush looked about him appraisingly, and chose a seat beside a tall leather-faced man in shirt sleeves.

"Sit down, buddy," said the man. "You're rocking the car. Sit down and lend me a match."

"My name is George Brush," said the younger man, seizing the other's hand and looking him squarely and a little glassily in the eye. "I'm glad to meet you. I travel in school books. I was born in Michigan and I'm on my way to Wellington, Oklahoma."

"That's fine," said the other. "That's fine, only relax, sonny, relax. Nobody's arrested you."

Brush flushed slightly and said, with a touch of heaviness "In beginning a conversation I like to get all the facts on the table."

"What did I tell you, buddy?" said the other, turning a cold and curious eye on him. "Relax. Light up."

"I don't smoke," said Brush.

The conversation did the rounds of the weather, the crops, politics, and the business situation. At last Brush said:

"Brother, can I talk to you about the most important thing in life?"

The man slowly stretched out his full lazy length on the reversed seat before him and drew his hand astutely down his long yellow face. "If it's insurance, I got too much," he said. "If it's oil-wells, I don't touch 'em, and if it's religion, I'm saved."

Brush had an answer even for this. He had taken a course in college entitled "How to approach strangers on the subject of Salvation"—two and a half credits—generally followed the next semester by "Arguments in Sacred Debate"—one and a half credits. This course had listed the openings in such an encounter as this and the probable responses. One of the responses was this, that the stranger declared himself already saved. This statement might be either (1) true, or (2) untrue. In either case the evangelist's next move was to say, with Brush:

"That's fine. There is no greater pleasure than to talk over the big things with a believer."

"I'm saved," continued the other, "from making a goddam fool of myself in public places. I'm saved, you little peahen, from putting my head into other people's business. So shut your damn face and get out of here, or I'll rip your tongue out of your throat."

This attitude had also been foreseen by the strategists. "You're angry, brother," said Brush, "because you're unaware of an unfulfilled life."

"Now listen," said the other, solemnly. "Now listen to what I'm saying to you. I warn you. One more peep of that stuff and I'll do something you'll be sorry for. Now wait a minute! Don't say I didn't warn you: one more peep—"

"I won't trouble you, brother," said Brush. "But if I stop, don't think it's because I'm afraid of anything you'd do."

"What did I tell you," said the man, quietly. He leaned over, and picking up the briefcase that was lying between Brush's feet, he threw it out of the window. "Go and get it, fella, and after this learn to pick your man."

Brush rose. He was smiling stiffly. "Brother," he said, "it's lucky for you I'm a pacifist. I could knock you against the roof of this car. I could swing you around here by one leg. Brother, I'm the strongest man that was ever tested in our gym back at college. But I won't touch you. You're rotted out with liquor and cigarettes."

"Haw-haw-haw!" replied the man.

"It's lucky for you I'm a pacifist," repeated Brush, mechanically, staring at the man's eyes, the yellow strings of his throat, and the blue stain his collar button had left.

By now the whole car was interested. The leather-faced man threw his arm over the back of the seat and included his neighbors in his pleasure. "He's nuts," he said.

Voices in the car began to rise in a threatening tide: "Get the hell out of here." . . . "Put him out."

Brush shouted into the man's face: "You're full of poisons— Anybody can see that. You're dying. Why don't you think about it?"

"Haw-haw-haw!" said the man.

The noise in the car rose to a roar. Brush went down the aisle and entered the toilet. He was trembling. He put his hand on the wall and laid his forehead against it. He thought he was going to throw up. He muttered over and over again, "He's rotten with liquor and cigarettes." He gargled a mouthful of cold water. When his breathing had become regular again, he returned to the car "Quarritch." He walked with lowered eyes and, sitting down, he held his head in his hands and stared at the floor. "I shouldn't hate anybody," he said.

16

BRUSH AT THE BANK*

Thornton Wilder

The bank consisted of one big room, high and well lighted, with a pen in the middle, walled in with a show of marble and of bright steel gratings. Beside the door the president sat in his smaller pen, filled with despair. Short of a miracle his bank had little over a week to live. Banks had been failing all through these states for months, and now even this bank, which had seemed to him to be eternal, would be obliged to close its doors.

Brush glanced at the president, but, resisting the temptation to go and talk to him, went to a desk and, drawing out his bankbook, made out a slip. He presented himself at the cashier's window.

"I'm closing up my account," he said. "I'll draw out everything except the interest."

"I beg your pardon?"

"I'll take out the money," he repeated, raising his voice as though the cashier were deaf, "but I'll leave the interest here."

The cashier blinked a moment, then began fumbling among his coins. At last he said, in a low voice, "I don't think we'll be able to keep your account open for so small a sum."

"You don't understand, I'm not leaving the interest here as an account. I don't want it. Just turn it back into the bank. I don't believe in interest."

*Abridged from pages 19-35 in *Heaven's My Destination* by Thornton Wilder. Copyright 1934, 1962 by Thornton Wilder. By permission of Harper & Row, Publishers.

The cashier began casting distraught glances to right and left. He paid out both sum and interest across the grating, mumbling: "I . . . the bank . . . you must find some other way of disposing of the money."

Brush took the five hundred dollars and pushed the rest back. He raised his voice sharply and could be heard all over the room saying, "I don't believe in interest."

The cashier hurried to the president and whispered in his ear. The president stood up in alarm, as though he had been told that a thief was entering the vaults. He went to the door of the bank and stopped Brush as he was about to leave.

"Mr. Brush?"

"Yes."

"Might I speak to you for a moment, Mr. Brush? In here."

"Certainly," said Brush, and followed him through a low gate into the presidential pen. Mr. Southwick had a great unhappy sheep's head rendered ridiculous by a constant fluttering adjustment of various spectacles and pince-nez and black satin ribbons. His professional dignity reposed upon an enormous stomach supported in blue serge and bound with a gold chain. They sat down on either side of this monument and gazed at one another in considerable excitement.

"Mm . . . mm . . . ! You feel you must draw out your savings, Mr. Brush?" said the president, softly, as though he were inquiring into an intimate hygienic matter.

"Yes, Mr. Southwick," replied Brush, reading the name from a framed sign on the desk.

". . . And you're leaving your interest in the bank?"

"Yes."

"What would you like us to do with it?"

"I have no right to say. The money isn't mine. I didn't earn it."

"But your money, Mr. Brush—I beg your pardon—your money earned it."

"I don't believe that money has the right to earn money."

Mr. Southwick swallowed. Then in the manner he had once used while explaining to his daughter that the earth was round,

107

he said: "But the money you deposited here, that money has been earning money for us. The interest represents those profits, which we share with you."

"I don't believe in profits like that."

Mr. Southwick edged his chair forward and asked another question: "Mm . . . mm . . . ! May I ask why you have thought it best to withdraw your money at this time?"

"Why, I'm glad to tell you, Mr. Southwick. You see, I've been thinking about money and banks a lot lately. I haven't quite thought the whole matter through yet—I'll be able to do that when my vacation comes in November—but at least I see that for myself I don't believe in saving money any more. Up till now I used to believe that you were allowed to have *some* money—like five hundred dollars, for instance, for your old age, you know, or for the chance your appendix burst, or for the chance you might get married suddenly—for what people call a rainy day; but now I see that's all wrong. I've taken a vow, Mr. Southwick; I've taken the vow of voluntary poverty."

"Of what?" asked Mr. Southwick, his eyes starting out of his head.

"Of voluntary poverty, like Gandhi. I've always followed it somewhat. The point is to never have any money saved up anywhere. Do you see?"

Mr. Southwick mopped his forehead.

"When my pay check comes every month," continued Brush, earnestly, "I immediately give away all money that's left over from the month before, but I always knew that at bottom that wasn't honest. Honest, with myself, I mean, because all this time I had five hundred dollars hidden away in this bank here. But from now on, Mr. Southwick, I won't need any banks. You see, the fact that I had this money here was a sign that I lived in fear."

"Fear!" cried Mr. Southwick. He rapped the bell on his desk so hard that it crashed to the floor.

"Yes," said Brush, his voice rising as the truth became clearer to him. "No one who has money saved up in a bank can really be happy. All the money locked up here is being saved because people are afraid of a rainy day. They're afraid, as they say, that worst may come to worst. Mr. Southwick, may I ask if you're a religious man?"

Mr. Southwick was deacon in the First Presbyterian Church and had passed a red velvet collection bag for twenty years, but at this question he jumped as though he had been struck sharply in the ribs. A clerk approached him. "Go out at the corner and get Mr. Gogarty at once," he commanded, hoarsely. "Get him at once!"

"Then you know what I'm talking about," continued Brush. His voice could now be heard throughout the hall. Clerks and depositors had stopped what they were doing and were listening in consternation. "There is no worst coming to worst for a good man. There's nothing to be afraid of. To save up money is a sign that you're afraid, and one fear makes another fear, and that fear makes another fear. No one who has money in banks can really be happy. It's a wonder your depositors can really sleep nights, Mr. Southwick. There they lie, wondering what'll happen to them when they get old and when they get sick and when banks have troubles—"

"Stop it! Stop what you're saying!" cried Mr. Southwick, very red in the face. A policeman entered the bank. "Mr. Gogarty, arrest this man. He's come here to make trouble. Get him out of here at once."

Brush faced the policeman. "Arrest me," he said. "Here I am. What have I done? I haven't done anything. I'll tell the judge. I'll tell everybody what I've been saying."

"Come on along. You come on quiet."

"You don't have to push me," said Brush, "I'm glad to come."

He was taken to the jail.

"My name is George Marvin Brush," he said, seizing the warden's hand.

"Take your dirty hand away," said the warden. "Jerry, get the fellow's prints."

Brush was led into another room to record his finger-prints and to be photographed.

"My name's George M. Brush," he said, seizing the photographer's hand.

"How are yuh?" said the other. "Glad to see yuh. My name's Bohardus."

"I didn't catch it," said Brush, politely.

"Bohardus—Jerry Bohardus."

Jerry Bohardus was a retired policeman with a kindly disposition and a dreamy, fumbling manner. A shock of long gray hair fell into his eyes. "Kindly step up in front of this glass table for me," he said. "It's fine weather we're having."

"Oh, fine," said Brush. "It's fine, outside."

"Now put your hand down lightly on this pad, Mr. Brown. That's the ticket. That's right. That's fine." He lowered his voice and added, confidently: "Don't feel badly about this business, Mr. Brown. It's just a form we gotta go through, see? It don't mean anything. They send these here prints to Washington, where there are eighty-five thousand others; some of them belong to sheriffs and mayors, too, yes, sir. I wouldn't be surprised if there were a few senators. Now the other hand, my boy. That's the ticket. So you never had this done before?"

"No," said Brush. "The other town I was arrested in didn't seem to care about it."

"Probably they didn't have the ay-paray-tus," replied Bohardus, complacently knocking the glass table with his knuckles. "We give two thousand dollars for all this, and it's a dandy."

Brush earnestly examined the result. "That thumb's not very clear, Mr. Bohardus," he said. "I think I'd better do it over again."

"No, that's clear enough. You've got a fine thumb. See them spirals?"

"Yes."

"They're just about the finest spirals I ever saw. Some say they stand for character."

"Do they?"

"That's what they say. Now we'll take your picture. Will you kindly put your head in this frame? . . . That's the ticket. It's funny about finger-prints," continued Bohardus, placing a board of numerals against Brush's chest. "Even if there were a trillion contrillion of them no two'd be alike."

"Isn't that wonderful!" replied Brush, his voice lowered in awe. Bohardus retired under a dark cloth. "Do you want me to smile now?" called Brush.

"No," answered Bohardus, emerging and adjusting his lenses. "We don't generally ask for a smile in this work."

"I suppose you've seen lots of criminals in your day, Mr. Bohardus?"

"I? I certainly have. I've bertillioned people that have killed their folks and that have poisoned their wives and that have spat on the flag. You wouldn't believe what I've seen. . . . Now we'll get your side face, Mr. Brown. . . . That's the ticket." He came forward and turned Brush's head. He took the occasion to ask, delicately, "May I inquire what they think you did, Mr. Brown?"

"I didn't do anything. I just told a bank president that banks were immoral places and they arrested me."

"You don't say. . . . Chin up, Mr. Brown."

"My name isn't Brown. It's Brush—George Brush."

"Oh, I see. Well, what's a name, anyway? . . . There, now I guess we got some good pictures."

"Do you sell copies of these, Mr. Bohardus?"

"We're not allowed to, I reckon. Leastways, there never was no great demand."

"I was thinking I could buy some extra. I haven't been taken for more than two years. I know my mother'd like some."

Bohardus stared at him narrowly. "I don't think it shows a good spirit to make fun of this work, Mr. Brown, and I tell you I don't like it. In fifteen years here nobody's made fun of it, not even murderers haven't."

"Believe me, Mr. Bohardus," said Brush, turning red, "I wasn't making fun of anything. I knew you made good photos, and that's all I thought about."

Bohardus maintained an angry silence, and when Brush was led away refused to return his greeting. The chief of police, Mr. Southwick, and other dignitaries were in earnest conference when Brush was led into the warden's office. At once he approached Mr. Southwick.

111

"I still don't see what was wrong in the things I said. Mr. Southwick, I can't apologize for a mistake I don't understand. I can see that you might feel hurt because I haven't a very high opinion of the banking business, but that's not a thing you can put me in prison for, and it's not a thing I can change my mind about, either. Anyway, all I ask is a fair trial and I think I can clear myself in half an hour. And I hope there are as many people in the courtroom as possible, because in these depression times a lot of people ought to know what Gandhi thinks of money."

The chief of police came toward him threateningly. "Now stop this foolishness!" he said. "Stop it right now. What's the matter with you, anyway?" He turned back to his men. "Jerry thinks this guy's screwy. Perhaps we ought to take him up to Monktown for some tests. . . . How about it, young fella? What's the matter with you, anyway? Are you nuts?"

"No, I'm not," cried Brush, violently, "and I'm getting tired of this. You can see perfectly well I'm not crazy. Give me any old test you like—memory, dates, history, Bible. I'm an American citizen, and I'm of sound mind, and the next person that calls me crazy will have to answer for it, even if I am a pacifist. I told Mr. Southwick that his bank and every other bank is a shaky building of fear and cowardice. . . ."

"All right, dry up, pipe down," said the chief. "Now looka here, Brush, if you aren't out of this town in an hour you get the strait-jacket and a six-months' sanity test upstate. Do you hear?"

"I'd like to take it," said Brush, "but I can't spare six months."

"Gogarty," said the chief, "see him to the depot."

Gogarty was a tall man with a great bony jaw and pale blue eyes.

"Boy, are you coming along quiet?" asked Gogarty.

"Of course I'll be quiet," said Brush.

After they had gone a number of blocks in silence Gogarty stopped, turned, and putting one forefinger on Brush's lapel, asked in a confidential tone:

112

"Say, boy, where did you get that idea about the Armina Savings Bank bein' shaky? Who told yuh?"

"I didn't mean that bank only. I meant all banks."

This answer did not satisfy Gogarty. Lost in thought, he continued to peer over his spectacles into Brush's face. Then he turned and stared up the street.

"Looks to me like there's a lot of people at the door of that bank now," he said. Suddenly he was roused to action. "Boy, you stick by me," he said. He dashed into the house before which they were standing. A woman was washing the dishes. "Mrs. Cowles," said Gogarty, severely, "as constable in this town I am obliged to use your telephone."

"Why, certainly, Mr. Gogarty," said Mrs. Cowles, nervously.

"And I'll have to ask you, ma'am, to go out on the front porch while I'm talking here."

Mrs. Cowles obeyed. When Gogarty had received a reply he said: "Mary, put on your hat. Do what I tell you. Go down and draw out all the savings, down to the last cent. And run. Only got half an hour. And don't tell nobody what you're doing."

He left the house with Brush and allowed Mrs. Cowles to return to her work. He again peered up the street, and deciding that his duty lay there, trusted Brush to reach the railway station by himself.

Mr. Southwick went home and lay down in a darkened room. From time to time he moaned, whereupon his wife, moving about on tiptoe, would rise and change the damp cloths on his forehead, whispering: "Sh, Timothy dear! There's nothing to worry about. You just take a nap. Sh!"

18

"THERE IS DANGER EVERYWHERE, AND MERCY TOO"*

Suzanne Britt

There are but three kinds of people in this world, according to some friends of Suzanne Britt—N.R.'s, O.R.'s, and A.R.'s (meaning, respectively, Non-Religious, Overly Religious, and Appropriately Religious). Intermarriage between the clans is a risky business, she observes, whether it involves A.R. and O.R. Catholics, A.R. and O.R. Jews, even A.R. and O.R. atheists. "Marry off an O.R. to an A.R. anything, and you will see the melting pot boil over in a matter of months or years, scorching everybody within miles of the messy melange." Britt offers a comic perspective on the eternal controversy which rages between the down-deeps and the merely dipped.

Two friends of mine, daughters of a Baptist minister, divided the world into three camps: folks of their acquaintance were N.R.'s, O.R.'s, or A.R.'s—meaning, respectively, Non-Religious, Overly-Religious, and Appropriately Religious. I was all ears and grins, having always been afflicted by a tendency to categorize, tempered by the uneasy conviction that such slotting is simple-minded and, therefore, evil. The sisters dubbed me an A.R., the status they themselves favored, knowing of both my need of God and my reluctance to show it

*Suzanne Britt's essay first appeared in the November/December issue (1985) of *Books & Religion*, published by the Divinity School of Duke University, and is reprinted with permission. © 1986 by Duke University.

much in polite circles. These women had little use for a third sibling, an O.R. who had fallen under her daddy's evangelical spell. About N.R.'s, the Baptist offspring had little to say, there being no way to leap from the mountaintop experience of a Baptist upbringing down to the flat, intellectual, rational wasteland of godlessness. My buddies, the A.R.'s in a family of O.R.'s, threw up their hands somewhere in mid-adolescence, admitted that God was God, and settled down to the hard task of making God palatable, manageable, appropriate. They poured the sweaty, bloodier side of Christianity into propriety, like Twinings into a bone china teacup.

The sisters had several ways of having their faith and rejecting it, too. They hung out with liberals and signed up for courses in counselling. They took an ironic tone toward the twice-born, the submissive, the sentimental, the charitable, the charismatic, the fundamentalistic, the evangelistic. They rolled their eyes a lot in church, never mind, of course, that they were usually *there* and not somewhere else. And they had an aversion amounting to amusement about all kinds of Baptist stuff: Wednesday-prayer meeting, foreign missions, Girls' Auxiliary, Royal Ambassadors, Women's Missionary Union, Baptist Training Union, Sunday-School quarterlies, the Broadman Press, revivals, the invitational hymns, the passionate rededication of one's life to the Lord, the overnight conversion, the two weeks at Ridgecrest, the Southern Baptist Convention, the issue of inerrancy, the way the verses dragged on in "Just As I Am Without One Plea." But there they were, still sitting in the pew, unable to turn this way or that, neither striding out the back door to suave secularity nor dancing up the aisle toward total commitment. It was a puzzlement, this being neither here nor there, neither hot nor cold, neither zealot nor persecutor, neither ancient nor modern, neither prophet nor pragmatist. Their daddy, one of those mean, mean, fundamental machines, with blow-dried hair and the charisma of a used-car salesman, shook his head at the two A.R.'s he had raised and drew ever closer to his favorite little girl—the O.R. of a haunted and screwball bunch.

I present the conflict as a Baptist issue, but that is both selfish and arrogant. The same schisms occur between A.R. and O.R. Catholics, A.R. and O.R. Jews, A.R. and O.R. atheists. Marry off an O.R. to an A.R. anything, and you will see the melting pot boil over in a matter of months or years, scorching everybody within miles of the messy melange. I, an A.R. Baptist, married into an O.R. family, members of the Church of God. This concoction of bat's wings and eye of newt and zucchini and mushrooms and a splash of burgundy and hog jowl and beef tenderloin and a pinch of puppy dog tail was unfit for human consumption. "If you can't stand the heat, get out of the kitchen," said Harry Truman. When the kitchen blew up, I got out, taking the advice of a good A.R. if I've ever seen one, a man who knew God's place and put Him in it.

But living in an O.R. clan gave me a good perspective on the eternal controversy raging between the down-deeps and the merely dipped. I heard plenty, for example, about the Holy Spirit, and grew properly fearful of never having chanced to meet this Being, this Comforter. I also learned that even among O.R.'s the down-deep is a sometime thing. The rest of the time, the church congregation ran up and down the aisles, frantically trying to give the impression of a deep-down experience. But many Sundays in that Church of God church, the shouts seemed tinny, the ecstasies mechanized, the smiles and tears push-button operated, the fervor ministerially induced—not God-inspired. In other words, I learned that an O.R. may be, in reality, just another A.R. in heavenly drag. And, *mirabile dictu*, I learned that A.R.'s can slip into something more fundamental in the twinkling of an eye, even if what they have slipped into is decidedly tasteless.

Within my own little A.R. family of upstanding Baptists, an O.R. suddenly reared his desperate head. My baby brother got born again, not from the outside and for show but from the inside and for what seemed like an eternity. The man was instantly unrecognizable: out went corny jokes about Catholics, Jews, and Protestants jockeying for position at the Pearly Gates; in came earnestness and urgency and witness; out went cigarettes and Wild Turkey; in came abstinence and Gator Aid;

out went tyranny and rage; in came peace and prayer. Nobody liked my brother anymore—he was such a bore.

But Time, that great worldly bearer of rust and corruption, got all over him eventually and brought our brother home to the A.R. haven of rational consenters: an occasional cigarette, a couple of beers from time to time, a daily and punctilious devotion read from the pages of *Open Windows,* a really hilarious impression of Jonathan Winters or Bill Cosby's Fat Albert. We were glad to have him home, but the dissonance lingers on. Will he Find It again? Will we, in his Finding, be lost to him? Will one of us Find It? Is Flannery O'Connor's Misfit divinely and uncomfortably right when he grumbles, "Jesus throwed everything off balance"? Is it the mission field or the church pew for us?

I watch the wind and know it goes where it will, blowing us down, soothing us, whipping us to action, dying away forever. It is the great horror of the O.R.'s that they will drift inexorably into the Appropriate. It is the secret terror and shame of A.R.'s that they will be swept away overly much into the Religious Tide, leaving behind rituals, proprieties, dignity, irony, wit and intelligent detachment from the yucky pot of salvation, redemption and spiritual cataclysm.

The dyed-in-the-wool A.R.'s probably have a tougher time, going from the wry, brainy, satiric, controlled, well-mannered attitudinal stance into the corny, emotional, humiliating slums of Jesus-freakery. From St. Augustine to T. S. Eliot to Thomas Merton, there is much to be overcome, much to be embarrassed about. For women, however, the problem of switching from A.R. to O.R. passes unnoticed, probably because women are *supposed* to be swept away, brought low, blown into ecstasy. We have always been nutty as fruitcakes, besotted and rich. But still, those women friends of mine, the A.R. daughters of a Baptist preacher, resolutely remain just plain pound cake, with a sprinkling, some Sunday, of powdered confectioner's sugar. They would be mortified to find themselves suddenly violated by the Holy Spirit.

When O.R.'s slip into Appropriateness, the change is gradual and, therefore, less shocking—a quiet story not likely to hit the pages of *Guideposts*. The O.R. turned A.R. surely feels, and guiltily, that something has been lost, never to be recovered. But by tempering spiritual fervor, O.R.'s have achieved respectability—surely a great comfort in times of trouble. Pride and arrogance, spiritual competition, tithing, regular church attendance, civic-mindedness—all the trappings of churchiness can protect these former O.R.'s from the searing memory of when they were brought low and raised up to new life. They manage. They become, in the end, pillars of the church, getting their names affixed to gold plaques, donating the church organ, underwriting air-conditioning and pew cushions, putting flowers on the altar, in memory of their dearly departed O.R. mothers.

I suppose the only categories into which all of us truly fit are the ones God forms in the secret places of our beings. We are sitting ducks for the bullet that comes out of the woods, in or out of season. We A.R.'s, O.R.'s and N.R.'s can't be too careful. There is danger everywhere, and mercy, too. And the last laugh will surely not be ours. This is the way the world ends, not with a sob, harrumph, or titter.

19

There are ways to be a successful pastor other than the conventional route of piety, hard work, and total dedication to one's congregation. The pseudononymous Charles Merrill Smith gives aspiring successful pastors advice in his popular How to Become a Bishop Without Being Religious. *Following these homiletical guidelines, anyone can preach like an expert.*

"HOW TO BE IMPRESSIVE IN THE PULPIT"*

Charles Merrill Smith

Unless you attended a really first-rate seminary, which is unlikely since there are so few of them, probably you have been taught that a clergyman's first, primary, basic, fundamental, highest, most sacred, most precious function, duty and privilege is to preach.

Chances are you have been dunked in the doctrine that you will ultimately rise or sink in your chosen work on the basis of your performance in the pulpit. Also, if you were so unfortunate as to fall under the spell of a persuasive professor of preaching with liberal inclinations, you may even believe that you should take some long-bearded Old Testament prophet as your ideal and denounce the supposed evils of our society as, for example, Amos whacked and lacerated the society of his day. This would certainly be a bad mistake. After all the only

---

*From *How to Become a Bishop Without Being Religious* by Charles Merrill Smith. Copyright © 1965 by Charles Merrill Smith. Reprinted by permission of Doubleday & Company, Inc.

pulpit Amos ever filled was at Bethel—and he was requested to resign after one sermon.

At any rate, the interpretation of the minister's role largely in terms of his preaching function is encouraged by the laity which supposes that the delivery of a weekly homily constitutes the clergy's major work load. You will get awfully sick of the jibe "Pretty good pay you get, Reverend, for working one hour a week." This is delivered always by the coarse, hearty type of parishioner who thinks it is original with him. It is best to smile if you can manage it.

However, if you care to achieve more than very modest success in the church, you must (1) convince yourself that all this business about preaching being your most important task isn't true and (2) convince your congregation that it is.

Let me elaborate. If you believe preaching to be first and most important in the work of a minister, you will naturally devote the largest slice of your time and energy to the preparation of your sermons, thus robbing yourself of the opportunity to address yourself to the genuinely vital and productive duties of your calling.

Any veteran cleric who has gotten anywhere at all will assure you that preaching is quite secondary in his scale of values. Yet we keep getting, year after year, floods of fresh seminary graduates who are enamored of the image of the pulpiteer. They buy an astonishing number of books. They use up the good working hours of the morning for study. They have a tendency to write out their sermons, polishing and repolishing them. And some of them even plan their sermons for the entire year ahead. This is expensive in terms of precious time and your meager supply of ready cash (books are frightfully costly these days). It is also entirely unnecessary.

However, your laymen should be allowed the illusion that preaching is your number one task because the illusion can be made to pay you rich dividends.

Fix firmly in the structure of your basic operating philosophy the fundamental fact about the ministry of the pulpit, which is: "It is ridiculously easy and requires but a negligible chunk of your time to be a popular pulpit personality."

Now if this is true (and rest in the confidence that it is), then it requires no especially gifted imagination to grasp the possibilities here. So long as your congregation is enthusiastic about you as a preacher, the following benefits will accrue to you:

1. The congregation will be inclined to charity concerning your weaknesses, and you are bound to have some. ("Well, we must remember that good pulpit men are hard to come by," they will say—a judgment which usually buries any criticism of your deficiencies.)

2. When your church members don't see you they will assume that you are sequestered in your study poring over the Scriptures, the philosophers, the post-Nicene fathers (they haven't, of course, the remotest notion of what a post-Nicene father is) adding to this intellectual sour mash the catalyst of your own reverent insights and thus distilling the spiritual booze which will give their souls a hearty wallop when you serve it up on Sunday morning. So long as they assume all this, they will not wonder how you spend your time, which permits you a considerable amount of personal freedom.

3. Your reputation as a superior pulpit man will get around, and better paying churches will be after you.

Now is the time, then, to perfect yourself in the skills of the popular preacher. No other professional investment will return such dividends on so small a capitalization. It is a situation comparable to having gotten in on the initial stock offering of IBM or General Motors.

The first rule for the popular preacher to remember as he prepares a sermon is that style is of enormous importance while content makes little ultimate difference in the congregation's enthusiasm for one's efforts in the pulpit. About 1000 parts style to 1 part content is a good proportion.

No one cares very much what you say when you preach, so long as it is not radically controversial or disturbing. Your acceptability as a preacher depends almost wholly on how you say it. A really gifted preacher can deliver an exegesis of "Mary

Had a Little Lamb" or extol the virtues of the single tax and send the congregation home in a spiritual trance, while a bumbler can bore it to death with a sensible and relevant exposition of the parable of the prodigal son.

All too few young clerics starting at the front door of their career trouble themselves to ask the question "What do my people want from a sermon?" Rather, they ask themselves "What had I ought to give my congregation when I preach?" Which is only another form of the question "What do I want to give them?"

Fundamentally, preaching at its best is one of the entertainment arts, and the successful pulpiteer will always think of himself first as an entertainer. His problem is much the same as Jack Benny's or Shelley Berman's or Mort Sahl's. He has to stand up and keep the customers interested in what he is saying or business will fall off at an alarming rate. The following chapters will examine the techniques of pulpit entertainment.

Entertain the customers

The old pros of the pulpit know that they should always aim to do three things for and to the customers (congregation) in every sermon:

1. Make them laugh
2. Make them cry
3. Make them feel religious

This does not mean that people in church should be induced to guffaw like drunks in a night club. The amenities of civilized churchgoing preclude this sort of congregational behavior. A preacher should not aim to be a belly-laugh comedian—but he should be a hearty-giggle humorist or he is unlikely to be called to a major league pastorate.

This level of skill is attained by loading the sermon with funny stories. They don't need to illustrate anything (one can always contrive to make a story fit); they just need to be funny.

The wise young clergyman, then, will early begin the habit of collecting funny stories. Buy books of them, clip them out of newspapers and magazines, paste them in scrapbooks or keep them in files. You can never have too many of them.

Let us now illustrate how to go about selecting a funny story for pulpit use. Let us suppose you are preparing a sermon on Christian missions. One of your points will likely be "The joys and advantages of being a Christian." Now when you come to this point in the sermon you can say, "Of course there are disadvantages to being a Christian. Sometimes people take advantage of the Christian's spirit of benevolence. This reminds me[1] of the story of the Jewish man who was converted to Christianity. After he was baptized and received into the church, he went home and was met at the door by his son who said, 'Pop, I need $5000 for a new sports car,' and his father gave it to him. As he came into the front room, his daughter came in and said, 'Father, I'm going to Europe and the trip will cost $5000,' so he gave it to her. As he went into the kitchen to see what was cooking, his wife said to him, 'Dear, I've ordered a new mink coat and it costs $5000.' So he gave it to her.

"Then, alone for a moment, he meditated on all this.

" 'Here I've been a Christian for a half-hour,' he said to himself, 'and these damn[2] Jews have taken me for $15,000 already.' "

Here is a nearly ideal humorous sermon illustration. For one thing, it does illustrate a point more or less. (And though we have previously noted that this is by no means necessary, it is a good idea to connect up your stories to the sermon wherever possible—and it usually is.) More important, it subtly reinforces your people in one of the prejudices to which they cling with tenacity and makes them feel comfortable about it.

You can be certain that any middle-class, standard-brand Protestant congregation is anti-Semitic. Not blatantly anti-Semitic, of course. You would get the gate in no time at all if you preached the Gerald L. K. Smith line. Also, hardly any of your

---

1. One is always "reminded" of a story in the pulpit, even though hours have been spent locating it and it is a part of the manuscript.
2. In less sophisticated churches substitute "darn" for "damn."

good people would admit to prejudice against Jews. It isn't popular to do so, and besides everyone wants to think he is tolerant. Most of your members even know and like some individual Jewish family. But to a person they think of Jews as avaricious, selfish, grasping and quick to take advantage of the other fellow. At the same time, they feel vaguely guilty about feeling this way.

So with this illustration, you have managed to imply (a) that Jews are actually like we all think they are, and (b) if Jews would only become Christians they would immediately become generous, warmhearted and unselfish like us, and (c) the Christian religion is demonstrably superior to the Jewish religion and, by implication, to all other religions.

So in this one brief story you have succeeded in extending permission to hold a prejudice, absolved the people of their guilt over holding it,[3] and have made them feel good about being Christian because Christians are superior people. And all this has been accomplished in the most entertaining of ways—through a funny story.

You cannot hope to turn up so ideal an example of the humorous story for pulpit use every week in the year. But if you keep it in mind as a model, it will help you in your selections and remind you to make the people laugh.

Make them cry

Now we come to the art of making them cry. Of course we do not mean that actual tears must flow (although if the custodian regularly comes upon damp discarded Kleenex when he picks up after the service, it is a heartening indication that you are consistently striking the bull's-eye). A lump in the throat and a quivering sensation in the breast, however, are quite adequate.

For making them cry, so to speak, your best bets are stories about old-fashioned virtures and values, patriotism and

---

3. Absolution of guilt has always been one of the first functions and duties of a priest.

self-sacrifice. If you tell them properly these will always do the trick.

Let us inspect a brief example of the lump-in-the-throat story.

A poor but scholarly and conscientious preacher has a little girl who desperately wants a new dress for an important party at the home of a wealthy parishioner. Her father sadly tells her there isn't any money for a new dress (build up his pain and anguish). She can't understand it, so finally her mother takes her into her father's study, points to the rows of books and says, "Darling, here is the reason there is no money for a new dress."

The point here which is calculated to open up the tear ducts is that the little girl must give up what all little girls have as an inalienable right to possess in order that her poor, struggling father may have the tools to do the Lord's work.

The story, of course, is full of logical holes. One could just as well conclude that her father sacrificed his daughter's welfare to his passion for scholarship. Why did he need all those expensive books? Why couldn't he have sacrificed a little for his daughter's sake? If his parishioners wanted a scholarly preacher, why shouldn't they pay the freight?

But be assured that your hearers will never even think of these questions. They will only feel sad and tearful over the plight of the little girl caught in the meshes of a necessary self-denial that a high and noble end may be achieved.

This story has the added advantage of a subliminal but persistent suggestion that the clergy bears the burden of great hidden expenses, which, you will discover, is all too true. It could easily produce a substantial book-allowance item for you in the next church budget.

You must not be too crude with the "cry stories," of course. Little Nell dying of malnutrition in the garret because Papa spends all the money at the saloon served her day, but the modern congregation, however plebeian, will not respond to it and might even chuckle—which would be disconcerting to you to say the least.

The untimely passing of a lovely young thing in the bloom of youth leaving behind a desolate and inconsolable lover is a theme with excellent possibilities so long as it is made clear that the love relationship has been entirely spiritual in nature. Turn the Lady of the Camellias into a church deaconess or a virgin schoolteacher and you will be amazed at the lachrymose response you will get.

Make them feel religious

Now we come to the problem of making them feel religious. This is the easiest of the three because it is mostly a matter of nomenclature. You need only employ a sufficient number of words and phrases which are loaded with "religious" meaning to accomplish the desired end.

For quick reference, the author here includes a brief lexicon of graded religious words and phrases. Roughly, a number one word or phrase has twice the religious punch of a number two and three times that of a number three.

LEXICON

Faith of our Fathers (1)

Bible-believing Christians (1)

Repentance (3) (Many people are not enthusiastic about repenting.)

Salvation (2) (A good word, but carries some overtones of the camp meeting.)

The Bible says (1) (Billy Graham's favorite phrase. Most congregations will believe anything you say if you precede it with this phrase.)

Christ-centered (1) (Use this often.)

Righteousness (3) (Given the lowest rating because it implies that Christians ought to behave themselves according to a standard stricter than many church members care to observe.)

God-fearing (1) (Your people aren't afraid of God, of course, but they enjoy thinking that they are.)

Serve the Lord with Gladness (1) (This has a fine biblical and literary ring to it, sounds as if you are calling for instant, forthright action, but is sufficiently vague as to require nothing at all from your hearers. Hard to beat.)

The Good Book (2) (Older members will like it, but it is a little dated for younger people.)

Sin (or sinners) (1) (Every sermon should include one or the other. These words conjure up images of bordellos and orgies and black lingerie—which images have an entertainment value in themselves. Your people will never connect the words with anything that middle-class white Protestants do, so you can flail away at sin and sinners to your heart's content.)

The Kingdom of God (1) (Your congregation has heard this phrase from every preacher that ever served them, so they consider it a true mark of a devout and stable minister.)

Holiness unto the Lord (1) (Not one member has a clue as to what this means but it is one of the most euphonious and soul-satisfying phrases in the lexicon.)

Heaven (1) (No preacher ever got fired for preaching about heaven so long as he made it clear that he thought everyone in his congregation would get there.)

Hell (3) (Just as well lay off this one or use it sparingly.)

These examples should suffice to give you the general idea of how to go about making your people feel religious. As a rule of thumb, rely heavily on those words and phrases which evoke pleasant religious feelings, and use with considerable economy any word which might make people uncomfortable or fidgety (which is why we warn against preaching about hell, for you would be surprised at the members of your flock who are trying to quash the suspicion that they might end up there).

Notes on noteless preaching

Let us now turn our attention to some do's and don'ts of preaching, little practical suggestions—each by itself a small thing perhaps—but put together adding up to great things for you so far as preferment in your calling is concerned.

At the top of the list of those items which you should do is this: Always preach without manuscript or notes of any kind.

Young clergymen seldom grasp the value of perfecting themselves in the "noteless" style of sermon delivery. Most of us have weak memories and feel horribly insecure without the comforting presence of a manuscript on the podium in front of us. Not one person in a thousand feels naturally inclined to this style of delivery. It is the very scarcity of noteless preachers which works to the advantage of the man who is one.

When you preach without notes, the focus of attention for the congregation is not your sermon but your performance. Since most of your listeners are paralyzed and inarticulate in front of an audience with everything they intend to say written down and before them, they are vastly amazed that anyone can stand up and talk for twenty minutes or so without visible aids to the memory, no matter what he says.

This situation obviates the need for undue concern over the content of your sermon since hardly anyone will be more than casually interested in what you say, thus lightening your preparatory labors and granting you many extra hours every week to do with what you please—hours which your less gifted brethren of the cloth will spend sweating over the manufacture of a manuscript for Sunday morning.

You may have observed already that the possession of a noteless preacher is a genuine status symbol for a church, the ecclesiastical equivalent of a chinchilla coat or recognition by the headwaiter at Le Pavillon. These confer status because they are rare, and rare status symbols cost quite a bit of money. This law operates just as surely in the ecclesiastical world as in the secular world, and a noteless preacher always commands a higher salary than even the most profound of his brethren who encumber themselves with manuscripts.

Those fortunate few congregations blessed with a noteless preacher become inordinately proud of him, and brag about him much as they brag about breaking 80 at golf or being invited to the Governor's for tea. They never comment that their preacher is learned or witty or forceful or devout or thought-provoking or inspiring. They always say, "You know, he preaches without a single note."

Also, the noteless style endears you to the extremely pious members of your flock who tend to be suspicious of written sermons on the grounds that excessive advance preparation allows insufficient opportunities for the workings of a divine inspiration. The extemporaneous homily seems to them to come from the heart instead of the head, and is thus a sure sign and seal that their preacher is "spiritual."

Since the pietists are a hard-core type of group in the congregation, sticking together like scotch tape and presenting a solid front in both their enthusiasms and their dislikes, it is a group to be reckoned with. A sensitive ecclesiastical politician can always smell an impending change of pastorates by sniffing the wind near the pietists of the congregation. If the pietists are voicing criticisms of their pastors, no matter how few and mild, the cloud no larger than a man's hand has appeared on the horizon and this pastor is well advised to start looking for another job, because the pietists will eventually get him. They are as relentless as Javert. Therefore, the wise pastor will learn how to cater to this group, and noteless preaching is one of the best ways to commend himself to it. Exhaustive research by the author has failed to turn up a single case of a noteless preacher falling into disrepute with the pietists of his congregation.

A preaching program which can't miss

As you begin your career of labor for the Lord, you must keep in mind that, while the content matter of your sermons is not too important if your style is adequate, there are some types of sermons which are almost guaranteed to win enthusiastic reactions from your congregation.

If you will never forget that your beloved parishioners are primarily interested in themselves, their spiritual aches and pains, their desire for whatever they equate with happiness, their urge to succeed socially and financially, the preservation of their provincial prejudices, then you will do the bulk of your preaching on these subjects.

One eminent New York preacher whose name escapes us at the moment (Freud would probably have been able to account for our forgetfulness) has become the best-known Protestant clergyman of our generation, has made pots of money and acquired all the good things which come the way of the sensationally successful preacher simply by remembering this one simple fact. Buy his books, hear him at every opportunity, and imitate him insofar as it is possible for you to do so and you, too, will hit the ecclesiastical jackpot.

Your people, you will discover, have an insatiable appetite for sermons on how to improve themselves or solve their emotional (spiritual) problems so long as the panacea you offer them does not require them to (a) quit doing anything they like to do, (b) spend any money or (c) submit to any very rigorous or time-consuming spiritual discipline.

What you need, then, is a formula tailored and trimmed to the above specifications. The author suggests that whenever you preach a "how to use the Christian Faith to get what you want" type of sermon (and you should be preaching just such a sermon eight Sundays out of ten) it is well to rely on a formula which varies no more than the rotation of the earth. The formula is this: Whether the sermon deals with the problem of loneliness, frustration, marital felicity, getting ahead in one's business or whatever, the solution to the problem is always:

(a) a catchy, easily remembered Bible verse (variable with each sermon according to the topic)
(b) a simple, sunny little prayer to repeat as needed (also variable, as above)
(c) an exhortation to have faith (this item is invariable. You don't have to be specific about faith—in fact, it is better if

you are not specific—just urge faith. Faith in faith is the best-selling item in your line of goods you will discover. There is very little sales resistance to it).

One obstacle you will need to overcome in training yourself to preach Sunday after Sunday on these "helping yourself through the Gospel" themes is the immense boredom you will suffer. Since you will be preaching essentially the same sermon nearly every Sunday, changing only the title, the text and the illustrations, you will find it difficult to convince yourself that your congregation will not be bored too. But it won't, and this you must accept as an article of your homiletical faith. No one has yet come up with a satisfactory explanation for this phenomenon. It is just a fact of life. Trust it and act on it.

The remaining 20 per cent of your preaching can be devoted, for the most part, to sermons for special occasions. These should be keyed to our more important national holidays. Many youthful clergymen, inspired no doubt by the highest and most pious motives, begin their careers by using the Christian calendar as a guide for their preaching. But the wise ones quickly discard this antiquated practice. The only days in the so-called church year which merit a special sermon are Christmas and Easter—and these merit it because they have evolved into important national, commercial holidays rather than for any vestigial religious significance still clinging to them.

Following is a month-by-month listing of the special days you will want to observe from the pulpit along with suggested themes for the day.

JANUARY

First Sunday—New Year's Day sermon. Topic: "Twelve Joyous Months With Jesus."

FEBRUARY

Sunday nearest Washington's birthday. Topic: "Faithful to the Faith of Our Nation's Founder." (This may be changed on alternate years to the Sunday nearest Lincoln's birthday. It involves only a slight change in the topic, which might be "Faithful to the Faith of Our Greatest President." The sermon can be substantially the same.)

MARCH

No particularly important special day unless Easter falls in March.

APRIL

Easter Sunday (usually). Topic: "Looking Forward to a Good, Old-Fashioned Heaven." (Do not forget to give the Easter-only churchgoers a thorough lacing for their failure to show up the rest of the year. This gives the regulars a sense of their own righteousness and spiritual superiority, and the Easter-only crowd expects to catch it from the preacher because they always have. They will not mend their ways, of course, but they hardly feel they have been to church if you fail to flay them.)

MAY

Second Sunday—Mother's Day. Topic: "Our Mother's Faith."

JUNE

Third Sunday—Father's Day. Topic: "Faith of Our Fathers."

JULY

Sunday nearest Fourth of July (might fall on last Sunday in June). Topic: "God's Chosen People." (Stressing, of course, that America and Americans are God's examples of what He expects other nations and other peoples to be like. This sermon may also be used at American Legion rallies and other patriotic occasions. It is a sure-fire hit.)

132

AUGUST

These are the dog days for church attendance. No special days. Better take your vacation in August.

SEPTEMBER

Sunday nearest Labor Day (could be last Sunday in August). Topic: "God's Labor Laws." (Point out that the laboring man needs to get back to the old-fashioned values of an honest day's work for an honest wage, and gratitude for the enterprising and risk-taking capitalist who makes his job possible. Express sympathy and concern for the good workmen of America caught in the evil grip of organized labor. Since you are likely to have few members of labor unions and lots of employers in your congregation, this will be one of the most popular sermons of the year.)

OCTOBER

Last Sunday—Reformation Sunday. Topic: "The Menance of an Alien Religion." (Reformation day isn't much of a special occasion in our churches, but it does afford an opportunity to whack the Roman Catholics. Since there is a mood of tolerance in the air, what with the late President Kennedy and the late Pope John, care must be taken to attack the still unpopular aspects of Roman Catholicism—the political aims of the Vatican, the mumbo-jumbo of its priestcraft, that sort of thing.)

NOVEMBER

Sunday before Thanksgiving. Topic: "God's Blessing Means God's Approval." (The theme here is that God has blessed America beyond the blessings of any other land, which means that God likes us best.)

DECEMBER

Christmas Sunday—Topic: "The Babe from Heaven." (There is simply no way to preach an unpopular sermon when you have a

133

baby, motherhood, heaven, humble shepherds and adoring wise men to talk about. Stick to the pageantry of Christmas. Beware of exploring the meaning of the Advent very much beneath the surface aspects of the story, for this can get you into trouble.)

Had this book been written a few years ago, the author would have issued an iron-bound injunction against any preaching which attempts to relate the Gospel to contempoary social issues. Nothing subtracts from the marketability of a preacher so much as having the label "liberal" pinned on him. Not many of us invite attacks on our theological orthodoxy these days because 94-44/100 of any modern standard-brand congregation is so theologically untutored that it wouldn't be able to recognize a heretic. It has no way of distinguishing between theological orthodoxy and heresy. But is it quick to spot any slight leaning toward liberal social views in its pastor. Heresy today is social rather than theological, and every congregation has its self-appointed Torquemadas anxious to oil the rack to heat up the fires around the stake.

It would be best, therefore, if the preacher could avoid entirely any reference to any subject which has a side to it capable of being construed as "liberal." The author can remember when church life had a lovely, serene, other-worldly flavor to it because preachers did not concern themselves with temporal problems. But this day has disappeared because we now live in unhappy times in which every newspaper brings tidings of some social problem which directly involves religion, the church and the faith and which forces us to make some kind of response.

It is, in fact, a decided advantage to you to be known as a fearless and forthright and prophetic pulpit voice—so long as you can achieve this reputation without being thought liberal. So you will have to venture out into the choppy and shoal-filled waters of preaching on social issues. There is no avoiding it, or the author would counsel you to do so.

The danger of being specific

This, then, is the most dangerous part of the preaching ministry. But if you will follow three simple principles, you can mitigate the dangers of shipwreck.

The first principle is this: Never be specific as to the Christian position on any burning social issue of the day.

For example, if you feel compelled by current events to preach on racial segregation, never, repeat, never, suggest that integration is the Christian solution. In fact, eschew the term "integration" entirely. It is far too specific.

The points you will want to make in this sermon will go something like this:

1. Extremism in racial matters is the chief evil.
2. The colored people ought to reflect on the great strides forward they have made and not be too impatient for too much too soon.
3. Brotherhood and Christian love will point the way. "You can't legislate love" is an excellent phrase to use here. (Since the congregation will define "Brotherhood" and "Christian love" to mean a kind of vague good will toward colored people so long as they stay in their place, they will take no offense at this.)

The problem here is to avoid any suggestion that white Protestant Christians have been at any point remiss in their attitudes or actions, and at the same time outline a solution which involves new attitudes and actions (since any idiot can reason that if what we have always done isn't working, we had darn well better think up something else).

This is a delicate but not insoluble dilemma for the preacher. The way out is to keep handy a set of non-specific words and phrases which allow the members of the congregation to fill in their own meaning. "Brotherhood" and "Christian love" have already been mentioned. It is always a good idea to urge your people to employ more of "the spirit of Christ" in the solution to social tensions, since hardly any of them know what this means but practically all of them think they do.

What you have working for you here is the average American citizen's touching faith in simple solutions to vast and complex problems. And people who believe that a balanced budget or bombing Cuba or a Republican administration would solve the problems of the nation and the world will have no difficulty believing that your non-specific phrases are clear Christian answers and that you are therefore a keen and courageous preacher.

A second principle to follow in preaching on social issues is to preach on problems which are as remote as possible from your community. You can denounce the government of South Africa with all the vigor at your command, but be careful about denouncing political corruption in your own city, because some of your good members might be involved. Criticize to your heart's content the Godless New York stage, but don't knock the local movie house, because someone in your congregation may be leasing it to the operator.

The third principle, and perhaps the one of pristine value to you in preaching on social issues, is to reverse your righteous indignation for those questions on which there is no substantial disagreement among your members.

As this is written, the Supreme Court ruling on prayer in the public schools is getting a lot of attention in the press. Since most of your people have been led to believe by the papers they read that the Supreme Court is systematically undermining the American way of life, they will welcome several sermons on "this atheistic decision." This issue should be good for several years yet. But by far the safest social problem on which the preacher may take an unequivocal position is the temperance question. You are aware, of course, that in the newspeak of the temperance movement temperance doesn't mean temperance. It means total abstinence from the use of beverage alcohol.

Your congregation is made up of members who advocate temperance and members who drink without apology, the proportions varing with the size, sophisitication and urban or rural character of your community. But both groups expect the preacher to trot out a temperance sermon every so often in addition to frequent blasts on the subject as a subpoint in other sermons. The temperance people love to hear you lambaste booze, and the drinkers are not offended by it because they understand that this just goes along with your job. A preacher who doesn't preach temperance sermons is as unthinkable as a Frenchman who frowns on love. This is the one social issue which involves no danger whatever, no matter how violent your denunciation.[4]

If you understand your people, their hopes and fears and prides and prejudices (and every truly successful pastor does understand these things), then all you need to do to be a highly regarded pulpit man is to tell them what you know they want to hear. After all, they are badgered and buffeted by worldly cares six days a week, and they need a sanctuary from all this on Sunday. They should be able to come to the Lord's house when the sweet church bells chime secure in the knowledge that they will find it here. They should come anticipating a jolly, sprightly, positive, entertaining, noncontroversial homily from their beloved man of God, aware that no discouraging or disturbing word will be spoken from your pulpit.

If your good people can count on this kind of preaching from you, you can count on their heartfelt appreciation expressed in their continuing affection, fulsome praise, a solid reputation as a fine pulpit man, and more tangible evidences of gratitude in the form of salary increases, better housing, and maybe a trip abroad for you and your wife with all expenses paid. Your true reward (apart from a perfectly legitimate joy in your professional success) will be, of course, the knowledge that you have served the Lord by comforting his people—and this is the knowledge which maketh glad the heart.

---

4. The author knows of three churches which realize a considerable amount of annual income from the leasing of property on which alcoholic beverages are dispensed. Yet the pastors of these churches continue to preach anti-booze sermons with, apparently, the complete approval of their congregations.

20

In autumn of 1965, Thomas J. J. Altizer, then professor at Emory University in Atlanta, shocked us with his so-called Death of God Theology. Many American Christians were shocked and outraged; few understood the complexities of Altizer's argument. Poet Anthony Towne responded, not in anger but in a piercing satire of the "death of God" theologians. He wrote a mock obituary for the "late God" which was reprinted in more than forty languages. It both admits the reality of the absence of God as a vital concern in modern life and the church (the Pope's reported absence from the funeral due to "the pressures of business"), and the absurdity of secular people proclaiming the death, in Georgia or elsewhere, of this "ultimate reality of Christians."

"GOD IS DEAD IN GEORGIA"*

EMINENT DEITY SUCCUMBS DURING SURGERY—SUCCESSION IN DOUBT AS ALL CREATION GROANS

LBJ ORDERS FLAGS AT HALF STAFF

Special to The New York Times

ATLANTA, GA., Nov. 9— God, creator of the universe, principal deity of the world's Jews, ultimate reality of Christians, and most eminent of all divinities, died late yesterday during major surgery undertaken to correct a massive diminishing influence. His exact age is not known, but close friends estimate that it greatly exceeded that of all other extant beings. While he did not, in recent years, maintain any fixed abode, his house was said to consist of many mansions.

The cause of death could not be immediately determined, pending an autopsy, but the deity's surgeon, Thomas J. J. Altizer, 38, of Emory University in Atlanta, indicated possible cardiac insufficiency. Assisting Dr. Altizer in the unsuccessful surgery were Dr. Paul van Buren of Temple University, Philadelphia; Dr. William Hamilton of Colgate-Rochester, Rochester, N.Y.; and Dr. Gabriel Vahanian of Syracuse University, Syracuse, N.Y.

Word of the death, long rumored, was officially disclosed to reporters at five minutes before midnight after a full day of mounting anxiety and the comings and goings of ecclesiastical dignitaries and members of the immediate family. At the bedside, when the end came, were, in addition to the attending surgeons and several nurses, the Papal

Nuncio to the United States, representing His Holiness, Pope Paul VI, Vicar of Christ on Earth and Supreme Pontiff of the Roman Catholic Church; Iakovos, Archbishop of North and South America, representing the Orthodox Churches; Dr. Eugene Carson Blake, Stated Clerk of the Presbyterian Church in the USA, representing the World Council of Churches, predominantly a Protestant institution; Rabbi Mark Tannenbaum of New York City, representing the tribes of Israel, chosen people, according to their faith, of the deceased; The Rev. William Moyers, Baptist minister, representing President Johnson; the 3rd Secretary of the Soviet embassy in Trinidad, representing the Union of Soviet Socialist Republics; and a number of unidentified curious bystanders.

Unable to be in Atlanta owing to the pressure of business at the second Vatican Council, now in session, the Pope, in Rome, said, in part: "We are deeply distressed for we have suffered an incalculable loss. The contributions of God to the Church cannot be measured, and it is difficult to imagine how we shall proceed without Him." Rumors swept through the Council, meeting under the great vaulted dome of St. Peter's, that, before adjourning the Council in December, the Pope will proclaim God a saint, an action, if taken, that would be wholly without precedent in the history of the Church. Several aged women were reported to have come forward with claims of miraculous cures due to God's intervention. One woman, a 103 year old Bulgarian peasant, is said to have conceived a son at the very instant God expired. Proof of miracles is a precondition for sanctification according to ancient tradition of the Roman Catholic faith.

In Johnson City, Texas, President Johnson, recuperating from his recent gall bladder surgery, was described by aides as "profoundly upset." He at once directed that all flags should be at half-staff until after the funeral. The First Lady and the two presidential daughters, Luci and Lynda, were understood to have wept openly. Luci, 18, the younger daughter, whose engagement has been lately rumored, is a convert to Roman Catholicism. It is assumed that the President and his family, including his cousin Oriole, will attend the last rites, if the international situation permits. Both houses of Congress met in Washington at noon today and promptly adjourned after passing a joint resolution expressing "grief and great respect for the departed spiritual leader." Sen. Wayne Morse, Dem. of Oregon, objected on the grounds that the resolution violated the principle of separation of church and state, but he was overruled by Vice President Hubert Humphrey, who remarked that "this is not a time for partisan politics."

Plans for the deity's funeral are incomplete. Reliable sources suggested that extensive negotiations may be necessary in order to select a church for the services and an appropriate liturgy. Dr. Wilhelm Pauck, theologian, of Union Seminary in New York City proposed this morning that it would be "fitting and seemly" to inter the remains in the ultimate ground of all being, but it is not known whether that proposal is acceptable to the family. Funerals for divinities, common in ancient times, have been exceedingly rare in recent centuries, and it is understood that the family wishes to review details of earlier funerals before settling upon rites suitable for God.

(In New York, meanwhile, the stock market dropped sharply in early trading. Volume was heavy. One broker called it the most active market day since the assassination of President Kennedy, Nov. 22, 1963. The market rallied in late trading, after reports were received that Jesus—see 'Man in the News,' p. 36, col. 4—who survives, plans to assume a larger role in management of the universe.)

Reaction from the world's great and from the man in the street was uniformly incredulous. "At least he's out of his misery," commentd one housewife in an Elmira, N.Y., supermarket. "I can't believe it," said the Right Reverend Horace W. B. Donegan, Protestant Episcopal Bishop of New York, who only last week celebrated the 15th anniversary of his installation as Bishop. In Paris, President de Gaulle, in a 30 second appearance on national television, proclaimed: "God is dead! Long live the republic! Long live France!" Mrs. Jacqueline Kennedy, widow of the late President, was reported "in seclusion" in her Fifth Avenue apartment. "She's had about all she can take," a close friend of the Kennedy family said. News of the death was included in a one sentence statement, without comment, on the 3rd page of Pravda, official organ of the Soviet Government. The passing of God has not been disclosed to the 800 million Chinese who live behind the bamboo curtain.

Public reaction in this country was perhaps summed up by an elderly retired streetcar conductor in Passaic, New Jersey, who said: "I never met him, of course. Never even saw him. But from what I heard I guess he was a real nice fellow. Tops." From Independence, Mo., former President Harry S Truman, who received the news in his Kansas City barbershop, said: "I'm always sorry to hear somebody is dead. It's a damn shame." In Gettysburg, Pa., former President Dwight D. Eisenhower, released, through a military aide, the following statement: "Mrs. Eisenhower joins me in heartfelt sympathy to the family and many friends of the late God. He was, I always felt, a force for moral good in the universe. Those of us who were privileged to know him admired the probity of his character, the breadth of his compassion, the depth of his intellect. Generous almost to a fault, his many acts of kindness to America will never be forgotten. It is a very great loss indeed. He will be missed."

From Basel, Switzerland, came word that Dr. Karl Barth, venerable Protestant theologian, informed of the death of God, declared: "I don't know who died in Atlanta, but whoever he was he's an imposter." Dr. Barth, 79, with the late Paul Tillich, is widely regarded as the foremost theologian of the 20th Century.

(There have been unconfirmed reports that Jesus of Nazareth, 33, a carpenter and reputed son of God, who survives, will assume the authority, if not the title, of the deceased deity. Jesus, sometimes called the Christ, was himself a victim of death, having succumbed some 1932 years ago in Palestine, now the state of Israel, purportedly on orders of a Roman governor, Pontius Pilate, and at the behest of certain citizens of Jerusalem. This event, described by some as 'deicide,' has lately occupied the deliberations of the Vatican Council, which has solemnly exonerated the Jews generally of responsibility for the alleged crime. The case is complicated by the fact that Jesus, although he died, returned to life, and so may not have died at all. Diplomats around the world were speculating today on the place the resurrected Jesus will occupy in the power vacuum created by the sudden passing of God.)

Dr. Altizer, God's surgeon, in an exclusive interview with the Times, stated this morning that the death was "not unexpected." "He had been ailing for some time," Dr. Altizer said, "and lived much longer than most of us thought possible." He noted that the death of God had, in fact, been prematurely announced in the last century by the famed German surgeon, Nietzsche. Nietzsche, who was insane the last ten years of his life, may have confused "certain symptoms of morbidity in the aged patient with actual death, a mistake any busy surgeon will occasionally make," Dr. Altizer suggested. "God was an excellent patient, compliant, cheerful, alert. Every comfort modern science could provide was made available to him. He did not suffer—he just, as it were, slipped out of our grasp." Dr. Altizer also disclosed that plans for a memorial to God have already been discussed informally, and it is likely a committee of eminent clergymen and laymen will soon be named to raise funds for use in "research into the causes of death in deities, an area of medicine many physicians consider has been too long neglected." Dr. Altizer indicated, finally, that he had great personal confidence that Jesus, relieved of the burdens of divinity, would, in time, assume a position of great importance in the universe. "We have lost," he said, "a father, but we have gained a son."

(Next Sunday's New York Times will include, without extra charge, a 24-page full-color supplement with many photographs, reviewing the major events of God's long reign, the circumstances of his sudden and untimely death, and prospects for a godless future. The editors will be grateful for pertinent letters, photographs, visions and the like.)

There has been as yet no statement from Jesus, but a close associate, the Holy Ghost, has urged prayer and good works. He also said that it is the wish of the family that in lieu of flowers contributions be made to the Building Fund for the Cathedral of St. John the Divine in New York City so that the edifice may be finished.

—**Anthony Towne**

21

In 1973, Marabel Morgan, fundamentalist Christian, became a publishing phenomenon with her book The Total Woman. *Millions of evangelicals were treated to Ms. Morgan's advice on sex and marriage. Critics labeled the book a "Kama Sutra for Christians." "Sex is as clean and pure as eating cottage cheese," announced Ms. Morgan. In order to put zing back into (marital) sex, she advocated new nighties, Saran Wrap, pink baby-doll pajamas, and white boots after baths.*

Martin E. Marty, University of Chicago professor and senior editor of The Christian Century *used one of his popular "M.E.M.O" pieces to fantasize about the results of some innocent fundamentalist putting Ms. Morgan's advice into action.*

"FUNDIES IN THEIR UNDIES"*

Martin E. Marty

THE SCENE: *A suburban doorway, 4 p.m. The door opens:*

THE TOTAL WOMAN: Help! Police! Rape!

THE TOTAL MAN: Shut up, I'm your husband!

TTW: Why are you wearing that mask, and your blue Spandex bikini underwear and those boots?

TTM: I have made "provision for the flesh, to gratify its desires" (Rom. 13:14).

TTW: You're adorable!

TTM: So are you. What gives with your white patent boots

---

and your passion-pink baby-doll nightie? Why the get-up at 4 P.M.?

TTW: I've been reading *The Total Woman,* by Marabel Morgan (Revell, $3.95). With 400,000 buyers last year, it's the best seller in hard-core.

TTM: Hardbound, not hard-core, you dummy. Let me in. I don't want spiels for books. I'm shivering. I want sex. Speaking of hardbound, I have the rope and whip.

TTW: Great! I am your slave; I am subject to my husband (Col. 3:18) as Marabel tells me to be; see also I Peter 3:1 and I Corinthians 14:34.

TTM: Stop spouting Bible verses. I want sex. What happened to your *Playgirl* magazines?

TTW: I threw them away since I became a Total Woman in the Lord. Marabel converted me. She shows how we fundies can have fun in our undies. Tie me up. Beat me. I'm your slave, as I said.

TTM: I like this Marabel Morgan. I'm glad you didn't read Galatians 3:28.

TTW: No! I adore your body. I crave your body. I worship your body.

TTM: Great! A little idolatry never hurt anyone.

TTW: I accept you. I adapt to you. I admire you. I appreciate you. Let's "plug into the Power Source" together, just like her book told us to.

TTM: Hold still while I'm tying you up. Say, why are you doing all this so willingly today?

TTW: Because Marabel told me what I'll get out of this. I have "set my affections on things above" (Col. 3:2), like airplane trips to Nassau. That's the gospel truth. I have "laid up for myself treasures on earth, where rust consumes" (Matt. 6:20). *The Total Woman* taught me to have a clean conscience while being sex-obsessed. And to be completely materialistic.

TTM: "The leech has two daughters: 'Give, give,' they cry. Three things are never satisfied; [including] the barren womb" (Prov. 30:15).

TTW: I'm not barren! I'm pregnant!

TTM: How can that be? Haven't you been using your pills each day?

TTW: But sweetie, that Valium makes me so woozy.

TTM: Now I'll really whip you!

TTW: Oh, thank you! I crave your body. I am subject to you in the Lord.

(The End)

Dear Reader: Are you offended by the explicitness of our drama? Does it strike you as a liberal permissive plot? Then read evangelical Marabel.

22

Robert McAfee Brown, professor at the Pacific School of Religion, was surprised to hear that Oral Roberts had a vision of Jesus, a vision of astounding proportions. In this satirical essay, he has fun with Roberts' claims.

"ORAL ROBERTS AND THE 900-FOOT JESUS"*

Investigating the Credibility of a Claim
from the Oral Tradition
Robert McAfee Brown

The noted evangelist Dr. Oral Roberts recently reported (a) that Jesus had appeared to him in a vision at 7 P.M. on May 25, 1980, (b) that the vision was "about 900 feet tall," (c) that he lifted the unfinished hospital Dr. Roberts is building high in the air, and (d) that he simultaneously promised that funds would be forthcoming to finish the structure.

This is an impressive series of assertions for a single vision, even if based solely on what might be called the Oral tradition, and they cover a wide range on the verifiability/credibility scale. Item (d), for example, seems beyond dispute, since after communicating the content of this vision to his followers by direct mail, Dr. Roberts received almost $5 million in donations, which works out to approximately $5,555.00 per foot of vision.

Item (c), that the hospital was lifted high in the air, is less easy to verify, although certain indirect evidence may be persuasive to some. If, for example, a mass of disconnected and multilated plumbing had been discovered on the ground floor of the partially finished building on the day after Dr. Roberts's vision, it could be argued that a sudden and unplanned levitation had been responsible. If, subsequently, bills from a plumbing establishment were received for "repairs to existing structure," this too would suggest that there had been an unusual disturbance in the building's location, and levitation could again be advanced as one among a number of possible hypotheses to account for the unanticipated repairs.

If, however, the pipes were plastic, it is conceivable that the extraordinary tensile strength of such products might have enabled them to withstand the sudden strain of being stretched beyond their original length. Thus we cannot arbitrarily rule out the possibility of levitation of the hospital complex, even if its plastic pipes still hold water.

I

But all of this is to cavil. The really challenging part of Dr. Roberts's vision is item (b), the 900-foot height attributed to the

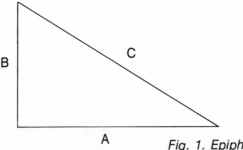

Fig. 1. Epiphany A.

Jesus of the vision. Our purpose in investigating this particular claim is not to ask the crass question "Did Dr. Roberts really see Jesus?" but to explore the more interesting epistemological question, "How did he *know* how tall Jesus was?" How, in the midst of such an epiphany (or "manifestation"), did Dr. Roberts ascertain the height of the one to whom we shall subsequently refer as the "epiphanic Jesus"?

Let us examine four possibilities:

1. The most obvious disposition of the problem is to assume that *the epiphanic Jesus told him so:* "I, Jesus, now 900 feet tall, promise you, Oral, now six feet one . . . " There are biblical references to Jesus' height that provide a precedent for such discourse. The evangelist Luke tells us that "Jesus increased in . . . stature" (Luke 2:52), and Jesus himself, speculating in the subjunctive mode, says, "And I, if I be [high and] lifted up from the earth . . . (John 12:32), although we must note in the name of academic integrity that the words "high and" are missing from some manuscripts. The latter verse, however, in its amended form just noted, may have been present in Dr. Roberts's subconscious mind, since the Alexandrian School has uncovered a variant reading that goes, "And I, if I be high and lift it up [sic] from the earth . . . "—thus adding biblical verisimilitude to the juxtaposition in Dr. Roberts's vision of (a) a tall Jesus (b) lifting an object up from the earth.

These theories, however, lack the real linchpin of a persuasive case, sharing as they do in the absence of any reference to the crucial number "900," or, to be really picky, any number at all.

II

2. Far more attractive, therefore, is a second theory which posits that Dr. Roberts's estimated height of the epiphanic Jesus was arrived at by *the geometric device known as triangulation.* If we know the length of two sides of a right triangle, we can, by squaring each number, arrive, with the help of a simple mathematical formula, at the square of the third side.

Thus, if Dr. Roberts was able to estimate the distance from where he was standing to the spot on which the epiphanic Jesus was standing, and if he was similarly able to estimate the distance from where he was standing to the top of the epiphanic Jesus' head, then he could easily ascertain the distance from the foot of the epiphanic Jesus to the top of the head of same, which would be, in lay language, his height. (See Figure 1, titled "Epiphany A," illustrating the well-known rule for right

150

triangles, viz, $A^2 + B^2 = C^2$, $C^2 - A^2 = B^2$, $C^2 - B^2 = A^2$.)

3. As a help in arriving at an estimate of the two necessary distances from which the third distance may be calculated, we must introduce a cultural factor known as *athletic transmutation*. We need to remember that in overseeing the construction of a huge hospital complex, Dr. Roberts is also the founder and president of Oral Roberts University, well-known for the prowess of its athletic teams. We can assume that the president of such an institution is well versed in the details of football, basketball and baseball, not to mention field hockey and water polo. Dr. Roberts would be well equipped, for example, to estimate distances in terms of their relationship to the length of a football field, known to be 100 yards, or 300 feet, in length.

Applying this information to the problem at hand, let us assume that, confronted with the epiphanic Jesus, Dr. Roberts cast his gaze horizontally along the ground, and saw that the feet of the epiphanic Jesus were, as he may well have said at the time, "about four football fields away" (= 400 yards = 1,200 feet). He then cast his eyes skyward (or, as he might prefer to say, "heavenward") and estimated the distance to the head of the epiphanic Jeus to be "about five football fields away" (= 500 yards = 1,500 feet).

Having satisfactorily completed these operations, Dr. Roberts then had at his disposal all the information necessary to arrive at the length of the remaining side of the triangle, which was, of course, the height of the epiphanic Jesus. Using the basic formula $A^2 + B^2 = C^2$ (see Figure 1, subtitled "Epiphany A"), transposed in this case to fit the data at his disposal, namely $C^2 - A^2 = B^2$, Dr. Roberts arrived at the following numerical transposition: $(1500)^2 - (1200)^2 = B^2$, or $2,250,000 - 1,440,000 = B^2$, or $81,000 = B^2$. Recalling that $\sqrt{81,000} = 900$, the height of the epiphanic Jesus can be calculated to be 900 feet or (in the unit of athletic measurement to which we have become accustomed) "about three football fields," or 300 yards. (See Figure 2, titled "Epiphany B.")

III

Here we must digress long enough to assure pious minds that there is nothing irreverent in establishing such a close connection between two seemingly unconnected entities; e.g., Jesus and football. We can do so by recalling that a few years

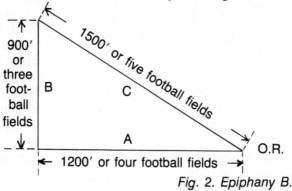

Fig. 2. Epiphany B.

ago Dr. Roberts, until that time an itinerant evangelist, was granted ordination in the Methodist Church, clear indication of the acquisition of an ecumenical mentality attuned to the relationship between divided Christian bodies. Such a step inevitably leads one even beyond Methodism (if the notion can be entertained at least for purposes of argument) into the central ecumenical arena known as "Protestant-Catholic relations" (or, as Catholics like to say, "Catholic-Protestant relations").

In building a library for his own university, Dr. Roberts would have studied the library plans of other universities, Catholic as well as Protestant. Confronting a large Jesus in a vision, Dr. Roberts's mind would inevitably have recalled *another* large Jesus, situated on the exterior façade of the library of the University of Notre Dame, a well-known Catholic institution, which has a representation of Jesus, many times life-size, both hands raised above the head in an act of blessing. Because the figure is clearly visible from the football stadium, it is known to Notre Dame football fans as "Touchdown Jesus," since the upraised hands, while indicating divine blessing to pious minds, also suggest, to minds profaned by the things of this world, the pose of a referee, hands raised over his head to indicate that six points have just been scored. The sequence (large Jesus → Notre Dame → football) is too obvious to need further commentary.

Converging evidence from the sacred science of numerology will quell any lingering skepticism about the vision under discussion. The vision occurred at 7 P.M., and 7 is a very mystical number, referring both to the seven gifts of the Spirit (cf. Isaiah 11:2, in the Vulgate translation), and the seven deadly sins. The vision occurred on May 25, the sum of whose two digits is 7, a very mystical number, etc. (see above). The vision occurred in 1980, the sum of whose digits is 18, the sum of whose digits is 9, which is the square of 3, the number for the Blessed Trinity, a celestial fellowship in which Christians believed the epiphanic Jesus shares.

The vision occurred on 5/25/80, and the product obtained by multiplying these numbers is 10,000, inevitably calling to mind the "ten thousand times ten thousand" of the heavenly host. The figure 900 is the square of 30, which equals the number of years of Jesus' life before the beginning of his public ministry. Most important of all: if we accept, as we must, the fact that Jesus was born in the year 4 B.C., we note that Dr. Roberts's vision took place 1984 years after Jesus' birth, and since "1984" is an Orwellian number suggesting many disasters for the human race, we can take the timing of the vision as a sure sign that divine countermeasures are already being instituted against that otherwise dread day.

IV

4. It would seem that our task is done. But we have not yet adduced the most significant evidence of all, having saved, after the manner of procedure at Canaanitic feast (cf. John 2:10), the best until the last. For after all, what is mere mathematical and athletic evidence, when compared to *biblical evidence?* Surely in the light of our subject matter, biblical corroboration would be more significant than mere secular reasoning.

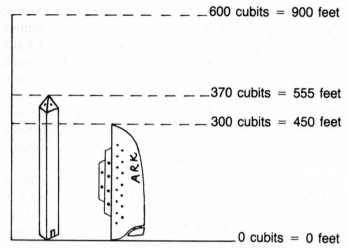

Fig. 3. Comparative Heights of Washington Monument and Noah's Ark.

(Note 1: The height of a 300-cubit epiphanic Jesus would be similar to the height of a 300-cubit ark, as explained in the text.)

(Note 2: The Washington Monument is on the left, Noah's ark on the right.)

We can arrive at persuasive biblical substantiation, but we must do so indirectly, posing as initial hypothesis about the state of Dr. Roberts's mind at the moment of vision, which, if it proves to be correct, will draw us yet closer to the truth.

Let us imagine Dr. Roberts at the point when his calculations have indicated "300 yards" as the height of the epiphanic Jesus. And let us hypothesize that at this very delicate point in the operation he suffered a momentary confusion over the most appropriate term of measurement to be employed, choosing finally to utilize a modern mode of measurement—i.e., yards—when, in faithfulness to Scripture, he should have employed a biblical mode of measurement; i.e., cubits. Appropriately fixated on the number "300," he should have concluded that rather than being 300 yards tall, *the epiphanic Jesus was 300 cubits tall.*

Let us observe how this helps to ensure the credibility of the vision. It is well known that a cubit equals two spans, or seven handbreadths, or 28 fingers. When we submit this incontestable data to a computer, we arrive at the discovery that a cubit is 17.49 inches, or approximately 18 inches. Let us now recall the ancient imagery of the early church which described Jesus as the new "ark of salvation," the one sure refuge in the stormy sea of life. And when, armed with this recollection, we turn back to the book of Genesis (cf. Gen. 6:14), and learn the dimensions of the original, or Noahic, Ark, we make a discovery of enormous significance.

The Noahic Ark, original symbol of salvation, was 300 cubits long, or, if stood on end, 300 cubits high (see Figure 3, titled "Comparative Heights of Washington Monument and Noah's Ark"). Thus if we are correct that Dr. Roberts's momentary lapse into a modern mode of measurement was simply an understandable (and surely forgivable) human error, and that when he thought the epiphanic Jesus was 300 *yards* high, the epiphanic Jesus was in fact 300 *cubits* high, we arrive at an epiphanic Jesus *exactly the same height as the ark.*

The symmetry of this equivalence between the old ark of salvation and the new is too striking to be coincidental. An epiphanic Jesus 300 cubits high is a perfect modern salvatory analogue for an ark of the same dimensions. It is too perfect not to be true, too unexpected to have been of mere human devising.

IV

As a further indication of the credibility of the vision, we may employ the ancient "argument from fitness." Let us take as a convenient norm for comparative measurement the Washington Monument, which is 555 feet tall in modern measurement, 370 cubits tall in a biblical universe. And let us, for purposes of discussion, divide people into two classes or categories, those (a) who are *taller* than the Washington Monument, and those (b) who are *shorter* than the Washington Monument.

We soon discover that we are not accustomed to seeing people who are *taller* than the Washington Monument, as a 300-yard Jesus would clearly be (see Figure 3). We are, on the other hand, quite used to seeing people who are *shorter* than the Washington Monument, and a 300-cubit Jesus fits easily within such a field of reference (see Figure 3, Note 1). And while we know that "with God all things are possible," as was said so well in Matthew 19:26, our credibility is tested to the breaking point by reports of a 300-yard Jesus, whereas a 300-cubit Jesus belongs within that class of persons whose existence we are most likely to accept without serious dispute.

If such an argument seems to diminish the stature of Jesus simply to that of other persons, let it be remembered that although he is in a class or category in which the rest of us participate, there are still few instances, if any, of individuals who come even close to a height of 300 cubits or 450 feet. So Dr. Roberts's claim if presented in cubits rather than feet seems more likely to be true than its contrary, but not so likely as to be merely ordinary. At all events, with the reduction of the height of the epiphanic Jesus from 900 feet to 450 feet, our difficulty in believing has been reduced by exactly 50 per cent, a figure quite in keeping with our conviction that a beneficient deity would meet us at least halfway along the road to our making an act of faith.

One and only one small numerical problem remains hovering over our entire exercise. It has to do with the claim of item (a), noted at the beginning of our discussion, that there was, in fact, a vision at all. The year of the vision, as we have already seen, was 1980. Now if, once again, applying the sacred science of numerology, we multiply the number $1 \times 9 \times 8 \times 0$ (a universally accepted method of determining the likelihood-factor in any proffered claim), the likelihood-factor at which we arrive by this exercise is zero.

Back to the drawing board . . .

156